Maidens' Trip

Maidens' Trip

A Wartime Adventure
on the Grand Union Canal

Emma Smith

BLOOMSBURY

LONDON · BERLIN · NEW YORK

First published in Great Britain in 1948
This edition published in 2009

Preface © Emma Smith 2009
Text © Emma Smith 1948

Photograph p. 226 © The Waterways Archive Gloucester
and reproduced by permission

The moral right of the author has been asserted

Produced under license from the Belmont Press whose edition
forms part of the Working Waterways series

Bloomsbury Publishing Plc
36 Soho Square
London W1D 3QY

www.bloomsbury.com

Bloomsbury Publishing, London, New York and Berlin

A CIP catalogue record for this book is available from the British Library

ISBN 978 0 7475 9896 1

10 9 8 7 6 5 4 3 2 1

Typeset by Hewer Text UK Ltd, Edinburgh
Printed in Great Britain by Clays Ltd, St Ives plc

The paper this book is printed on is certified by the © 1996 Forest Stewardship
Council A.C. (FSC). It is ancient-forest friendly. The printer holds
FSC chain of custody SGS-COC-2061

Mixed Sources
Product group from well-managed
forests and other controlled sources
www.fsc.org Cert no. SGS-COC-2061
© 1996 Forest Stewardship Council

FSC

This book is dedicated to my mother, Janet Laurie

Preface to the New Edition

M*aidens' Trip* is part fact, and part fiction, and no-one has ever been quite sure which heading it ought properly to come under.

When, fairly soon after leaving the 'cut', I began to write the book, it seemed to me that the best method of describing the couple of years I had spent working narrow-boats on the Grand Union Canal towards the end of the Second World War would be to condense them into a single trip. For this imaginary portmanteau trip I invented as my two companions Nanette and Charity. I also, for the sake of balance and objectivity, exercised the novelist's right by largely inventing the third member of the trio, named as myself; (sixty years on I deny ever having been bossy). All the things that happen in the story to these three young fictional or semi-fictional characters did actually happen to actual girls, but over a much longer period of time and to a number of different girls.

Today the old boating families live ashore, and the GUC is a thoroughfare for pleasure-boats. But in 1943, when I was signed on by the Grand Union Canal Carrying Company under their wartime scheme of employing women to make use of boats lying idle, the Canal was still a commercial waterway. At that time steel was the cargo most usually carried north from London to Birmingham, although there were a good many variants, one of the nastiest being cement. Nobody liked to be given cement for their loading-orders. Not only did it disagreeably clog the eyes, lungs and hair during loading and unloading, but it also had to be kept dry in transit, and to keep it dry the bilge-pumps had to function, and for the bilge-pumps to function the bilges had to be free of coal, which they seldom were since it was with a cargo of loose coal that the boats were filled to their gunwales on each return journey. This southbound cargo, picked up in the region around Coventry, was shovelled out directly on to the wharves of factories purpose-built alongside the canal somewhere back in the vicinity of London.

It was, I remember being told, the peculiar directness of the canal pick-up and delivery system that more than compensated for the apparently anachronistic slowness of this means of transport. Monkey-boats ran in pairs with one boat, powered by a Diesel engine, towing the other, its butty. And, certainly, chugging mildly along the winding cut at approximately four miles an hour did seem to be a slow way of getting anywhere in comparison to the lorries that could be seen whizzing by on distant roads and the trains that went thundering past. But it was a case of the tortoise and the hare. The round trip took us greenhorns between two and three weeks to complete, depending on circumstances. Boaters did it in considerably less time.

To passengers glancing out of train windows, that four-miles-an-hour snail-crawl along the motionless stretches of water between lock and lock must have given the impression of an existence poetically timeless. It was a false impression. Time, in fact, was unceasingly crucial on the cut. Each and every day was, for the boaters, a race against time. When the loading-orders were issued at the depot office in Hayes, Middlesex, the boaters raced each other to cast off and get away first, so as to be the first to arrive in the docks, and therefore the first to be loaded, and the first to head north. Blackout regulations forbade the use of headlights for anything except the navigation of tunnels in daytime, but the boaters must have had eyes that could see in the dark; how, otherwise, did they manage to let go so early on winter mornings – and to keep going so late at night? Sunday was not a day of rest. The quicker they got to Brum, the quicker they would be unloaded and able to take on another load and be back at the depot to collect their pay and their new loading-orders, and be off again. They were paid by the trip. The family was a working unit, kids included, and whatever they were paid, they all earned it; but I don't think it made them very rich.

We strove, we newcomers, to emulate the boaters and to work the same unrelentingly long hours as they did. It was pride, though, not financial necessity that drove us on for, unlike them, we were paid a flat minimum weekly wage – a very small one. I remember listening to a reasonable explanation of the smallness: it would have been unfair for trainee girls to be given more money than the boaters earned, and not in our own interest, either, to arouse ill-feeling by being better paid since we relied on their goodwill to help us whenever we were stuck in the mud or in some similar fix. Of course we didn't want to be unfair or greedy – what a shocking idea! – and we quite saw the sense of not antagonising our essential sources of aid. For the two years I was on the cut I belonged to no union. I hadn't the slightest idea in those days what purpose a trade union served – indeed, I had scarcely ever heard the term.

The advent of war made, I think, very little difference to the boaters; they lived in a sort of permanent emergency situation anyway. Nor were they touched by the one undeniable benefit of war, its socializing effect. A boater was always on the move; on the move, moreover, with wife, children and the kitchen stove: he and his home, perpetually passing through a land – his land – of which he knew nothing, regarded by its inhabitants, his fellow countrymen, as a colourful curiosity.

Movement isolated him from this unknown outer world; illiteracy completed and sealed the isolation. Few boaters could read or write. How, or when, were they to learn these skills? Their children went to the depot school during brief periods when the boats were held up at Hayes, either for repairs or else because there was sickness aboard, or a birth under way. Such random bouts of education formed the only official schooling the boaters, those dignified uncommunicative people, ever had.

The war brought one difference, though, to them as to everyone else, and that was bombs. 1944 was the year the doodle-bugs were being sent over from the Continent, and the job of taking the boats down to the docks for loading and away again was like an adrenalin-fuelled dash in and out of Tom Tiddler's ground. Nobody wanted to get caught for the night in Limehouse Basin. It was said, and probably with truth, that if a bomb were to drop in the basin every boat lying there would be sucked under and sunk. When it came to air raids there was an advantage in having a home and work that moved; bombs, for the boaters, were only an occasional risk. But the London dockers, lock-keepers, and bargemen with their immense horses, worked daily in an area that remained static on the enemy's map, and went home at night, each one, to an irremovable house, built of bricks – a house eminently destructible.

All these men were linked in their various livelihoods by water. But between the house-dwellers and the boaters there was an unbridged gap, a kind of social silence. To us, counted as house-dwellers too, the dockers and bargemen were unreservedly friendly. I remember how grateful I was to be treated by them as a genuine working-girl, what a sense it gave me of being liberated from my upbringing. We didn't deserve to be treated so, for the truth was this: when we, the middle-class trainees, had had enough of dirt and cold and wet and bugs and bad food, we could walk away from it all without a backward glance; and everyone else on the cut, those with whom we rejoiced to mingle on equal terms, couldn't.

The wartime scheme to take on women in place of men had a limited success. There was never much more than a handful of girls on the GUC at any one time. Some stuck it, but in general the turnover was rapid. Accidents, not surprisingly, were frequent; the wonder is that none was fatal. It was all too easy for the inexpert, winding a paddle or leaping down from the side of a lock, to break an arm or a leg – it was even proved possible to crack a skull while steering the boats into a bridge-hole. Apart from these natural-selection accidents, the number of trainees was maintained at a low level by those girls who changed their minds after the first trip and decided to join the boating Wrens instead.

Maidens' Trip was my first book. I wrote it at top speed, in about three months, a year or so after the end of that war which we thought then had defeated fascism for ever. I was jobless and penniless, but full of unbounded hope. It was the mood of the time – in the streets, at any rate and I like to think that, more than six decades since its original appearance, readers of this latest edition of *Maidens' Trip* may get a whiff of the youthful exuberance and the confident belief in all good things being possible which are even more vital today if we are really to win, at last, a better world for everyone.

And in consideration of this new century's growing concern regarding climate change, I would like to add as a final word an urgent plea for putting to far greater use the national asset that we already possess. Our existing network of inland waterways offers us a viable alternative to the transportation of goods by road or rail, and one that would surely be environmentally preferable.

Emma Smith
London, July 2008

1

I t must have been an astonishing imposition for the canal people when war brought them dainty young girls to help them mind their business, clean young eager creatures with voices so pitched as to be almost impossible to understand. It must have been amazing, more especially since the war changed their own lives so little, for they read no newspapers, being unable to read, and, if they did possess a wireless, seldom listened to the news. For years, for generations, they had worked out their hard lives undisturbed, almost unnoticed. Then suddenly – the war; and with it descended on them these fifteen or so flighty young savages, crying out for windlasses, decked up in all manner of extraordinary clothes that were meant to indicate the marriage of hard work with romance. For the most part the boaters took it stoically. They watched narrowly, in silence, and they spat and they waited.

How gladly we abandoned our sex. How noisily we proclaimed ourselves 'like men' – the ancient cry we were resolved to render true. What an emancipation seemed to be ours. For at eighteen one wanted to be either a man or a woman, and to have been instead only a girl was a disappointment that lasted several years. Yes, how we welcomed our rough translation, and in what a little, little time we began to dream of laces and ribbons and underclothes made of chiffon.

1

Tilly took the three of us, Nanette, Emma and Charity, for our first trip – Tilly who, after a varied career which included ballet-dancing, had now at a thirtyish age given her heart generously, fanatically, to the Inland Waterways. She was dressed, invariably, in bell-bottom trousers, ear-rings and a peaked ski-ing cap. Very small, very tough, with a voice that came somehow manfully out of her stomach and a sailor's roll, she lived in mortal terror of offending the boaters for whom she would, at any moment, have spent her blood in battle. And because she was so whole-heartedly their lover, they liked their Tilly.

She observed us closely to judge whether our over-all reaction was towards or against our new life; for if it was against, we should never make good boaters, and if it was towards, we might. After only a few days it was plain we were losing the niceties of the landsmen. There was no nonsense about curling our hair at night, nor did we boggle at adopting a bucket for a lavatory, and the canal for a sewer; nor later remember this when it became expedient to wash our hands and feet in water scooped out of the cut. We took to it all with happy ease, for we were then in the last stages of our teens, an elastic age, and Tilly warmed towards us. She introduced us to her most prized friends; she explained to us as we passed from one beer district to another the merits of the different brews, and we listened gaping, for beer was a new and not wholly pleasant taste in our mouths. She crowned our happiness by saying we were her best pupils.

Her praise was murderous. We nearly killed ourselves to justify it, pooh-poohing the idea of changing our clothes after a heavy thunder-storm, struggling on that extra hour when splitting backs cried out for rest and gentleness. Blisters were nothing. Indeed, we admired our mangled hands beyond all decency, and if jealousy ever bared its yellow teeth it was only because at night, when the sodden clothes were put aside, Charity's body was found to be more savagely bruised than Emma's. Happy days of hell and hardship – how soon they passed. Almost as soon, it seems from this distance, as the bruises faded and the hands toughened.

At the end of three weeks we thought we knew it all. They gave us six days' holiday to take a bath, and on the seventh day we arrived back at the depot: Nanette, who was rich, Emma, who was bossy, and Charity, who was nothing in particular but probably the most agreeable of the three. Our kitbags were stuffed with clean shirts, our hearts were fixed on the peculiar glory of becoming accomplished boaters.

The end and starting-point of every trip was the lay-by, flanked on the one side by a heterogeneous collection of sheds, buildings and wharves at a point where the canal makes a sharp division, one arm branching off at right angles to reach eventually the Regent's Canal Docks – 'Limehouse,' as it was more tersely and generally known – and the other continuing onwards down to Brentford.

The lay-by itself was no more nor less than a spacious bed for boats, achieved very simply by a long strip of concrete, studded every few feet with an iron ring, to which rings the boaters tied up the sterns of their craft. The boats lay packed together as close as herrings on a dish, chimneys smoking, brasses gleaming, a squall and a buzz of life rising off them all the time like steam from a pudding, and the reversed up-curving tillers of the butty-boats indolently waving from side to side with each spasm of water. Paint was bright and liberal. On every side the sunshine was overstocked with the brilliant colours of a merry-go-round, scarlet and blue, white and glossy black. Roses were painted on the water-cans, castles on the cabin doors, and round the wooden helms and along the sides of the boats just above highwater mark were scattered sundry small geometrical designs such as children make with compasses in their first exercise books.

Although this street of boats seemed at a glance to be always the same, it was, in fact, always changing. Unlike a street, its houses moved. The women who scrubbed their washing and screamed at their menfolk were different from day to day, though this might at first be hard to realize: the dark faces and plaited hair could have belonged to a family of sisters, and the habit of ear-rings and long black cotton skirts and leather belts made individual identity even more perplexing. The men all wore corduroy trousers with a flap in front and choker scarves and went to bed in their shirts – so much we quickly learnt. But we were frightened of them, in particular of the women, who seemed so strong and never, like us, wore trousers. We mistook their taciturnity at first for dislike. We were wrong: they understood us as little, or less, than we understood them, and our conventions – such, for instance, as the one of talking more fast and freely when nonplussed – were unknown to them.

It was Vi Potter who first showed us the inside of a boater's cabin. The apartment, ten foot by six, with odd corners of stove and beams reducing it even more, was divided in two by lace curtains, looped elegantly up and dropped, we understood, at night, when her mother and father went to sleep behind them. Lace frills edged the shelves and various pieces of hand-made lace were also tacked wherever there were a few inches not already occupied by horse-brasses polished to mirror brilliance, uncouth Victorian prints, photographs of married relations, the frames overlapping one upon the other, and an immense quantity of china plates. It was plain that space, in any form, was shunned, and haste made to do away with it. This was in keeping, after all, with the whole condition of living in a boat.

In a cabin of that size six people were just able to sit, and a cabin was intended only for sitting, and, at night, for sleeping. One stood on one's feet necessarily when climbing down into a cabin, and at that awkward moment when one clambered out. In the Potters' butty-boat cabin lived several children, Mr. and Mrs. Potter, and a family of chickens, amongst them a cock. In contrast to this undeniable crush, Vi had the motor-boat cabin to herself.

She showed us her book, from which, by her own effort, she had taught herself to read, and was now teaching her small brother. This book was a 1908 volume of *Punch* which she had bought in a second-hand clothes shop in Birmingham. The pictures left her unsmiling but she read out the words for us accurately without commas, stops or sense, and how she had taught herself to repeat them was a marvel and a mystery.

The lay-by was the harbour of enforced idleness. Here the boats waited till loading orders came through, or repairs were made, or sickness cured. Here, in the cramped and stuffy cabins, the boaters' wives gave birth to numerous babies, little creatures who would pass their early days chained for safety to the chimney-pots, and later grow into the wiry elderly-faced children who spend their childhood patiently trotting the miles of tow-path between London and Birmingham, standing on their toes to wind the lock paddles and gravely pushing open the hundred-year-old gates.

This lay-by was to become, in a sense, our home – a home in which we were not immediately at ease; we were shy, anxious to disprove ourselves as ladies, and very much afraid we were disliked. This had the effect of making our approach insincere and servile, though sincerity was our whole desire and friendship with a boater, the plum that each of us secretly sought. We had much both to learn and unlearn, amongst other things that a joke had to be simple almost to the point of being primitive, and that a boater, although he never said 'thank you,' would remember a kindness or a gift – or for that matter, a story or a joke – to his last day.

To one side of the lay-by was the township that served it: the paint-shop, the forge, the dry-dock, the stores, the carpenter's shop – the offices and canteen of the landsmen who worked to keep the boats afloat. Between the two groups, landsmen and boaters, existed a wary friendliness, an observance of the wide difference that divided their natures and their callings. The canal was their common bond, the old dirty cut, by and on which they lived, and for the which they gave their strangely devoted service.

We were presented with two newly-painted boats with old leaks, the *Venus* and the *Ariadne*, for our maiden trip. Canal-boats, such as ours, ran in pairs, one of them having a motor and towing the other, the butty-boat, which, having no engine, was therefore without power of its own. The *Venus* was our motor-boat, the *Ariadne* our butty.

Overcome with pride, we planned our furnishings on a scale extravagant, impractical and, in short, impossible. But in the first flush we hammered up six-inch curtains of red and white check across the single port-hole, and, with the object of keeping in touch with culture, nailed post-cards of National Gallery masterpieces to the yellow-varnished interior. Charity, for the same good reason, brought along her gramophone with records of Handel's Water Music and a Beethoven concerto, and these were soon sat upon and smashed to pieces and the bits scattered like the ashes of Bohemia on the stale waters of Stoke and Fenny Stratford.

We spent one day collecting all we hoped we needed in a fever of ill-balanced confidence, flying from paint-shop to smithy, making and losing lists of equipment, splicing, with our inexpert fingers, the stiff new cotton-lines, checking over, oiling up, duplicating and hindering one another until the evening found us exhausted and our nerves in a fine state of desperation.

'Now do you think,' said Emma at supper, as we spread our knees with greasy paper and stuffed our mouths with chips, 'that we've got everything? Have we got enough rope?' Rope was our obsession: with us it broke so easily.

'No one ever has enough rope,' said Charity, 'but we'll get some more as we go along.' She meant: steal. Rope, and how to steal it, was one of our chief pre-occupations, and rope, once stolen, our chiefest pride.

Nanette said: 'Oh, I forgot. I meant to tell you – do you know we've got bugs?'

'No. Nonsense. Impossible, Nanette. The boats have just been painted.'

'I tell you – I was sitting on the bucket this afternoon reading the paper and a bug – you can't mistake a bug – walked across the page in front of my eyes. Don't be silly, bugs aren't afraid of paint, they hide in cracks and make eggs and come out again twice as many when it's all over. I dare say,' said Nanette, 'they're only in my cabin at present, but I'm bound to bring them over with me.' Nanette was mistress of the motor-boat cabin, Emma and Charity sharing the larger one in the butty-boat.

'Well I do think, Nanette, you ought to learn how to make a Primus work, so that you can have tea and things in your own cabin sometimes. It's absurd to be dependent on us for all your meals and drinks.'

'I know quite well,' said Nanette, cramming her mouth with fish, '*how* to make a Primus work. I'm just afraid of it, that's all. I don't see why I should have my face blown off, and I should have it blown off because I'm bad with stoves, as you know very well. Don't be beasts,' she said, looking uneasily up through her fluffy hair at our solemn faces, 'I'll fill the water-cans instead if you like – always.'

She was hoping, we knew, that we were not going to be prim about her, and we were dubious and silent because already she hated tinned milk in her tea and had shown laziness about the early mornings.

After that we scrawled hurried letters homeward, under-lining 'wonderful' and dwelling on 'filthy,' and then, assuring one another that we could hardly be dirty having had baths only the day before, we crawled between our Army blankets and quickly went to sleep.

2

The morning was clear, frosty, sunny, sparkling. Nanette was in time for breakfast and we ate in a sickly silence, remembering that by evening we should be lying in the docks, and aware of the many locks and adult traffic and accidents that lay between now and then. Tilly, our teacher, was fifty miles out of ear-shot, dealing with a bunch of newer pupils. Truly we were on our own.

Nanette rolled up her sleeve and showed us the uneven outline of a bite nothing but a bed-bug could have raised.

'That's only one,' she said, scratching at her waist and bosom. Silence and fear.

Hammering came from the direction of the workshops; children were shouting hoarsely, boots clumped by on the concrete. Someone began to whistle aboard the next-door boat. The loud-speaker burst into an unpleasant kind of music, halted, cleared its throat, and called out in a monster voice:

'Steerer Smith, you're wanted in the office please, you're wanted in the office.' Then on with the music almost before our faces had time to blanch.

'Us,' cried Emma, leaping up, as best one could leap in that very small space. 'It's us; we're off.' And she muffled her throat in a red scarf and reached blindly round for her cap and was out of the hatches and off down the tow-path in less time than Nanette took to cut herself another slice of bread.

'Because we might as well eat while we can,' she said to Charity, with a certain amount of foreboding in her voice.

Emma joined a handful of boaters who waited outside the office and stamped up and down as they did, and, like them, she humped her shoulders and said nothing. One by one they were absorbed inside, and every few minutes out they came one after the other, with papers in their hands and a destination in their eye. In went Emma.

'Your boats ready?' said the sharp little man, holding one hand over the mouthpiece of a telephone and seeming still to listen to the sounds that came from its other end.

She nodded. She could hardly bring herself to frame what was almost certainly a colossal lie.

'Limehouse,' he said. 'Steel billets – new lot in from the U.S.A. Get going as soon as you can, they want to be rid of it.'

He gave her a trip-card and money and loading orders and a number of prettily pink cards with 'North Bound' printed across them; and he remembered, just as she was leaving, to say: 'Your first trip alone, eh? Be careful now.'

Nanette was at the blacksmith's collecting windlasses. They came clinking out from the fire, blue and rough, good enough for hardening off the hands, quite good enough for losing. We lost them by the dozen. The bottom of the cut must be strewn with those mouldering right angles of iron that we clutched so hard and lost so often; they fell from our fumbling hands and from the snug nests against our stomachs as though bewitched. We wore our belts in cowboy fashion, strapped low down round our hips, and, after the classical manner, carried our windlasses tucked in the front of them, supporting our stomachs like corsets. The boaters, on the other hand, carried theirs with thoughtless brilliance, anywhere, anyhow, and rarely lost them: in the small of their backs, dangling from a trousers pocket, hitched around their necks. The handles were silvery and smooth as glass from years of usage, and some of them were bound in brass.

10

With the windlasses jangling in her hand Nanette visited the paint-shop. Here the ceiling was hung with giant water-cans painted in bright colours, and she asked for two, a can for each boat. Stanley hooked them down for her like a Father Christmas in a bargain basement.

'Manage?'

'Yes, thank you.' Nanette dropped the windlasses. Stanley picked them up.

'Now those are new cans mind, not old ones done up. So take care you chain them. Don't you come to me at the end of the trip and ask for more.' Stanley knew his girls and their feather-brained way of driving boats beneath low hanging branches, so that when, once clear of the trees, they bobbed their cowardly heads up, chimney-pot was flat and water-can gone.

'Oh, we'll *chain* them,' swore Nanette, clutching cans and windlasses to her pillowy front. The cans slipped. She dropped a windlass. Stanley picked it up for her.

'No wonder you lose them,' he said, looking at her reproachfully.

In the carpenter's shop her rosy face was greeted with whistles drowned in the screaming of electric saws.

'I want some wedges,' she shouted, smiling at everyone. 'Put them in my pocket please.'

Old Victor stopped beside her, a plank across his shoulder. 'I'd like to take you out one of these nights,' he said, 'Somewhere posh, eh? We'd have a time, you an' me together, eh? Lights and dancing and music. But a girl's got to be careful, ain't she now?' He looked at her over his spectacles, crafty and wizened. Nanette was pleased.

Charity was just struggling aboard with the batteries. 'Help me,' she said. 'My stomach; my God. It must be awfully bad for us.'

Together, grunting with the weight, they bundled a battery into the engine-hole and hoisted it on to the shelf. The second

11

one stayed in the butty cabin under the side-bed and every few days it had to be changed with the other to charge anew off the engine.

'I like everything about boating,' said Charity to excuse herself, 'except batteries. They are so heavy. I worry about my inside, and hope it's all right.'

Emma arrived, fluttering the papers.

'Now are we all ready? We ought to go. I suppose everyone's watching us.'

We untied the sterns, simulating composure. Everybody was indeed watching us, but not with the malicious criticism we imagined. Their interest was mildness itself. Charity wobbled up to the bows and poised herself anxiously there, looking back the seventy-five feet at Emma.

'All right: untie.'

Charity unlashed the two bows and stood by to hand the two short lengths of rope to Emma as the motor-boat passed. She crouched like a runner, leaning forward. Her brows were knotted together with nervous anticipation. The motor-boat nosed out into the fairway and Emma came abreast.

'Now. . . .'

She snatched at one rope, gave it a hurried tug and crammed the eye of it over a stud on the motor deck. The butty-boat gave a gentle jerk and prepared to follow behind like a led horse. At that moment the motor-boat buried its nose firmly in the weed and rushes of the opposite bank, and both boats halted. The engine ticked over in an inquiring intelligent way, like a spaniel wondering what its master means it to do.

'Charity . . . where's *Nanette*?'

But Charity, her dark hair streaking behind her, was already half way up to the bows of the motor-boat, wrenching free a long shaft as she passed; throwing ashore one end of this she fell upon the other end like a Roman on his sword, and pressed and pushed with all her weight, the muscles of her arms almost bursting holes in her sweater with mortified effort. The boats

12

were unresponsive; they stirred not an inch, not a quarter of an inch. The scarlet blood rose and coloured Charity's face. Flickering in the corner of one panic-stricken eye was a bargehorse tramping steadily nearer, dragging a lighter loaded down with timber. The boats were right across its way.

'Emma,' she screamed. 'You fool – you've got the engine ahead. Reverse it, reverse it.'

Emma reversed the engine. The motor-boat answered at once to Charity's shaft and drifted to one side as easily as a leaf blown across a puddle. Charity clutched at the bows of a moored boat and held the *Venus* steady till barge and horse were by. The boaters, deeply interested, continued to lean in their hatches, waiting for the next act.

Much upset, Emma was just about to make a second attempt, when a young semi-bearded boy who was called, she later discovered, Eli Blossom, leapt aboard the deck of the *Venus* and silently relieved her uncertain hands of gear-wheel and tiller-handle. He was masterly, amazing Emma. We were out, we were free of the lay-by, released, blessed, even, one might believe from that single gesture, beloved, and heading for the docks. Our spirits lifted up in glory. The sun was brilliant. Our hair blew. We tore at five knots through broken blinding water. And Eli stepped off backwards on to a passing lighter as though the thing he had done was nothing. But he was divine, we knew. So we waved to him and boldly worshipped.

Five minutes passed like this, when, being drunk with Eli, we were in no condition to miss Nanette. Then we missed her. She was in neither cabin. She was not aboard. We had left her behind. We looked at one another, observing on each opposing face the dazzle of success die away.

'Well, don't go on,' said Charity, 'we're getting further from her every minute.'

'I'm not going back for her. I couldn't turn these things round if I tried. I'll go on the mud and she'll have to run. After such a good start – we're losing hours.'

We were too glum for fury. Mud and gravel scraped along the bottoms of the boats. We grounded and lay idle.

Presently we saw in the distance Nanette's short plump figure, well-bolstered up with overcoats and jerseys, flapping along at a great rate. When she saw we waited for her she began to walk. She was painfully out of breath when she finally reached us, but not in the least guilty. Her hair, with wind and hurry, was muddled together into a babyish tangle, her face was bright pink. We greeted her with bitter womanish looks.

'I do think,' she said at once, panting but severe, 'that you could have waited just five minutes for me. You must have known I wasn't on board.'

'No, we didn't. How could we possibly? You were on board a minute before. You knew we were going. Where were you anyway?'

'I went to the office lavatory for a treat. I couldn't shout that out to you, could I? But I never dreamed you'd start without me.'

'Well, never mind,' said Emma. 'Now you're here let's get on for goodness sake. Shove the bows out; it's half past ten.'

The butty, being tied closely behind, needed little or no steering. Emma took charge of the motor and the two others disappeared into the butty cabin to warm their hands and make themselves cocoa. It was agreed that if anything unexpected happened, Emma should blow her horn. For an hour or two the countryside streamed by unchecked on either side. Now and again we met boats coming up from the docks low down in the water with the weight of their cargo, and peaked with shiny black tarpaulin. Once loaded, the two boats were divided by a tow-rope seventy-five feet long, called a 'snubber,' and the steering of the butty became an arduous and unrelaxing vigil, needing strong arms to row at the tiller and a sharp eye. According to the custom, Emma slowed down on sighting a pair and crept civilly past them with a single stern nod of greeting.

To one steerer she called out: 'Are there many boats down there?'

He answered: 'Ah,' and she was hardly wiser.

The beat of the engine, the bubble of churning water, filled Emma's head. The noisy buoyant progress revived her wounded confidence and restored her temper. Hands in pockets, nose blue in the wind, eyes narrowed against the darting sunlight, she gazed ahead and rashly dreamed of Birmingham, that distant Mecca. The water, ploughed apart by the *Venus'* bows, dashed itself stormily against the shallow banks of the canal creating joy and danger for the children who scampered alongside and waited, shrieking, at every inlet for the waves to wet their feet. Dogs followed, barking. We passed a golf-course and men standing on the green in grey flannels shaded their eyes to watch us. We passed a factory and girls ran to a window to wave, and a man, high up, leaned out to shout: 'Hi, Blondie.'

We passed open fields and stunted trees and an avenue of limes. There were aeroplanes in the sky, and clouds and struggling birds. The *Venus* rounded a bend and bore down on a group of office workers eating sandwiches and drinking tea in the open air. Seeing this, Emma blew her horn and Charity bobbed up her scared face.

'I say – what about some cocoa for me?'

Nanette presently arrived with a slopping mug.

'What time do you think we'll get to Limehouse?'

'Oh, I don't know. Quite early I should think, at this rate.' Foolish, fatal words.

'What's that?' said Emma, peering ahead. We were nearing a bridge.

'I don't know. I can't see. Oh – slow down a bit. It's a barge coming through.'

'Well then, why isn't it *coming* through?'

15

As we approached it became obvious that the massive barge, much overloaded with timber, was stuck. We dropped speed to a minimum and crawled up to the bridge-hole. A fat man in a greasy cap laconically received us.

' 'Ullo girl,' he said to Nanette.

'What's happened? What's the matter?'

'Too much stuff aboard. Not enough water to float her through.' His mate was kneeling on the tow-path squinting down the crack between barge and bank. The horse waited moodily.

'Would you like a cup of cocoa?' said Charity, coming along.

'Well, if you got one going. Hi Ted. Warm your hands girl,' he said to Nanette who had already scrambled down to the steel deck of the lighter. 'Might as well make yourself comfortable. We won't get free of this, we won't, not for a long time.'

There was a brazier glowing aboard; Nanette politely spread her hands above it.

'What are you going to do?' she asked.

'Well, I dunno. That depends. Ted, have you give Rosie her dinner?'

His mate hung a nose-bag round the horse's neck and joined us, beaming. He was about thirty-four, with innocence making beautiful his clear blue eyes and ginger bristles half-concealing the mouth of a charmer.

'Don't you listen to what Charlie tells you,' he said to Nanette, 'He's a menace he is, a terror. He's an 'ome-breaker, that's what he is.'

Charity came up with mugs of cocoa and we all gathered round the brazier. It might have been Christmas or a carol-singing party. Emma thought it time that somebody worried.

'How long are we going to be stuck here do you think?'

'Difficult to say. Now don't you fret, girl. It'll be all right.'

16

Ted was saying to Charity: 'Of course my name's Edward but they call me Ted. I got a son called Leander. Time I'm telling you about, we was living in a house alongside the cut, and that morning the lady helping my wife looked out the winder just as I was passing. "Hi," she says, "you got a son, Ted," she says, shouting it out. "That's nice," I says. "Tell the missus we'll call him the same as this barge." We did too. Leander, he's called, same as the old barge I was on that morning.'

'Ah, Rosie's a wonder,' Charlie was saying to Emma, 'believe it or not, I've had 'er wiv me now for nearly seven year. I wouldn't change 'er, not for any other 'orse on the cut. She's got more sense than most chaps has. Eh, Rosie?' he called, and the horse flung up her head and glared round with wild eyes.

'D'you like dancing?' said Ted.

Charity nodded.

'I'm mad about it,' he said, leaning cosily back against the timber. 'Now my wife, she doesn't like it. Rather stay at home and sew and listen to the wireless. I had a dancing-partner once, an 'arf-breed girl. But she was' – he searched for the word exact and gave it to Charity emphatically, closing up his eyes – 'she was *nice*. And dance – you should have seen her. We went out dancing together every Saturday night for six years. Then I thought I was getting a bit, you know, fond of her. So course we had to stop. She was upset, she was, poor girl. Well, I was sorry.'

'Well now,' said fat old Charlie, smacking down his empty cup and rubbing his mouth, ''Ow about giving us a pull?'

Rosie was stirred from her dinner-bag and led clear of the bridge-hole. Ted fastened the end of a rope to the bows of the *Venus*, twisted it loosely round a stud on the deck of the barge and stood ready.

'All right,' he shouted to Emma. 'Take her away.'

The *Venus* backed, reverse gears whining shrilly. The rope ran loosely out. Then, with one quick turn, the rope was checked, the *Venus* took the strain. At the same moment Rosie with terrible cries and slappings was urged forward. There was a short time of battling endeavour. Then the *Venus*, her engine still fiercely hammering, slipped uselessly sideways. Rosie was allowed to relax.

'Never even shivered,' said Tom. 'She's fast all right. Come on now, let's 'ave it again.'

By this time we were playing to half a dozen people gathered on the tow-path and a number of children. A further audience leaned above us, over the bridge, transfixed with curiosity. The rope was attached. Rosie was lined up, the *Venus* put into reverse. Everyone, on or off the canal, helpfully strained his muscles.

'Hi,' shouted Charlie. Rosie, trailing her broken cotton-line, blundered into a canter. Several men began to run half-heartedly after her. With hellish cries the children followed Charlie. Ted rolled himself a cigarette and shook his head.

'Have to get a tractor I reckon,' he said.

'Let's have dinner,' said Charity. 'How lucky it isn't our fault.'

'What lovely men,' said Nanette, as we ate our eggs and bacon.

The afternoon passed pleasantly enough, for we were harassed by no responsibility. A tractor was fetched from the nearest farm, and later loaded boats arrived from the docks and lent their power in pushing. Several ropes were broken, and between each attempt long discussions took place, helped by cigarette-rolling, foot-shifting, and little promenades from one end of the barge to the other. Rosie had been recovered from half a mile up the cut and brought back to crop the grass and rest herself. The bystanders swelled and decreased but never altogether dispersed. The clouds closed up; a little rain fell. Then the sun shone again, but brokenly, as though discouraged by the wind, which was colder with a touch of evening in it. Charity kept a kettle continuously boiling and issued mugs of tea to everyone with dramatic generosity.

By four o'clock two or three further pairs of boats had arrived, both loaded and empty, and were drifting about on either side of the bridge. No one complained. It was accepted; it was even perhaps, in a sober head-shaking way, enjoyed. By four o'clock the men had begun to unload the barge, plank by plank. By four-thirty there was a pile of timber lying jumbled like wreckage on the tow-path, and the barge had moved a foot. Fifteen minutes later she floated free, was dragged by Rosie a few yards further up the cut, and there moored for the night. The boats, untangling themselves, the one from the other, engines banging and popping, exhaust smoke twirling on the wind, prepared to pass in orderly procession under the bridge.

'I think we ought to let them all go on ahead of us,' said Emma, 'even though we were the first. We don't want to make them cross or hold them up.'

So we were the last to go under the bridge, and the last to arrive at Camden Town Locks, and the last to tie up there, and little gratitude we got for it. Unselfishness is not a virtue understood by boaters. They thought we were fools, and so indeed we were.

3

Emma was woken up before the morning by rain falling coldly on her face through the open slide of the hatch. She rolled out on to a wet floor, and then standing on the step of the coal-box struggled vainly to close the slide. Being swollen and sticky, it jammed half-way. A stream of water, dislodged by her tugging, dived against her warm neck and unkindly trickled its way down inside her pyjamas. Finally she had to climb fully out into the darkness and rain to give one straight furious pull which closed the slide with a bang and woke Charity.

'Nothing,' said Emma. 'It's raining, that's all.'

She slid herself down inside the comforting cocoon of bedclothes and lay for a few minutes listening to the sharp patter of rain on the wooden roof of the cabin.

At half past six it was raining, if anything, harder. Nanette arrived for breakfast looking excessively plain under the drooping eaves of a sou'wester. She also wore an oilskin and gumboots.

'You're a fool if you run about in those things,' said Emma, looking at the boots. 'There's nothing more slippery in the wet.'

'I shan't run about,' said Nanette calmly, engaged at the same time in a life-and-death struggle with the sleeves of her oilskin over a slice of bread and marmalade. The once-trim stove, now splashed with orange rust, had a shabby appearance. Drops of water had sneaked through at the top of the bulkhead and were beginning to roll tentatively down the wood towards Charity's rumpled blankets.

'I wonder if all the boats leak,' she said, bundling her bedding together before it was overtaken by flood, and pushing it into the cupboard where it reposed during the daytime. 'Or do you think they give us the leaky ones on purpose? What a mean trick. Still, I don't suppose it matters,' she added doubtfully.

With the slide shut the cabin was a good deal darker, and it seemed smaller too, crammed with the stiff discomfort of oilskins, and other special equipment we had prepared for just such a day as this: mackintosh gloves and bicycle leggings. The boaters, we discovered on emerging much hampered by these anti-rain garments, were not concerned with rain or how to withstand it. Their hats were pulled a little closer over their eyes; otherwise their dress was unaltered and their expressions undismayed. With mugs of tea spitting and hissing on the cabin-tops in front of them, they waited for the lock-keeper to come and unchain the gates and let them through.

With the utmost difficulty we squeezed our bulky persons along the narrow gunwale and dropped down into the engine-hole. There we stood, bunched together round the brass cocks and green paint, while Emma primed the engine. Our understanding of this engine was rudimentary, and continued so throughout our dealings with it. What exactly this business of priming, performed religiously night and morning, did to help it along, we never knew. We went through the motions taught to us of starting an engine, and usually the engine started. This morning, to surprise us, it did not. Nanette and Charity bent, crackling, over the starting handle. Together they swung it round three times and at the third swing Emma pressed down the lever, known, in ignorance, as the jigger. This was the moment when our engine should have sprung to life, and the steel walls begun to shiver with its vibration, and a jet of water gone plopping out of one side into the cut. Nothing like this happened. Only the handle, too soon released, gave a vicious kick, just failing to rupture Nanette, she said.

'It must be cold. It is colder to-day. Come on, again.'

'One . . . two . . . three . . . . Now. . . .'

'Nanette,' said Charity, straightening her back, 'you're not trying. That time it was all me.'

'I can't see,' said Nanette, looking pitifully up from underneath the fallen hood of her sou'wester.

'Well, take that silly thing off.'

'I can't. It's got in a knot. You have a go instead,' she said to Emma.

There was a tiresome operation of changing over, in which Charity, who flattened herself against the bulkhead to be out of the way, got generally knocked about without complaining. Nanette pushed her sou'wester far back on her head, and, looking very determined, stood ready by the jigger. Overexcited, she pressed it down before the third swing, and was most angrily rebuked.

So it went on, exhaustion and ill-temper increasing with every minute. Altogether it took us just over a quarter of an hour to bring the engine alive. By that time the gates had been unlocked and the first pair of boats, one taking the right hand lock and the other the left, had sunk down out of sight and sailed away. Two further pairs of boats, loaded from the docks, were just rising up on the rising water.

'Quick,' cried Emma. 'We're next. Is everything ready? Are you ready both of you?'

The water levelled itself; the beams rocked slightly with a movement of relief, and the gates were pushed slowly open. Slowly, one before the other, the boats emerged and slid away past us, and left the full lapping water of the lock for us to profit by. The *Venus* and the *Ariadne*, strapped abreast, edged forward till their bows bumped the farther end, and the gates were closed behind them.

Bargemen were beginning to arrive. They wore sacks round their shoulders, and they spat out wet cigarette ends, and hunched themselves up and stamped their feet and swung their arms with no pretence at ignoring the weather. Little sympathy lay between them and the boaters. The boater carried his house about with him, and slept in a different place each night. The bargeman, who tied his craft up at the end of the day and went home to a solid house, accordingly reckoned him a gipsy, a wrong the boaters were not able to forgive. For ourselves, we found the bargemen affable and easy-tempered, very ready talkers or shouters, and behaving themselves with a most marked independence.

'Well, how do you like this bleeding rain?' said one of them kindly to Nanette, who, having wound herself a paddle, was now sitting on the end of a beam waiting for the water to sink and struggling to undo the knot in the strings of her sou'-wester.

'I don't like it very much,' she answered, swinging her short legs to and fro with the pleasure of being spoken to. 'Do you think it's going to stop soon?'

'Stop? Wot, this? Nah. Go on for weeks, this will. You'll have to take to swimming, girl, it's the only way to keep dry this weather.'

The horses on the tow-path shifted their great weight patiently from one side to the other. Their brasses jingled. Their towropes lay slack in the mud. There was a smell of wet dung and exhaust smoke and hay. On the bridge that arched above the locks, London buses ran their curving course, like messengers of another world. And the white faces that, every few minutes, halted on their way to limbo to peer over the side, seemed as remote and insignificant as news of dead relations. The thought of the dreary day they were surely just beginning filled Nanette with triumph instead of pity. Already she was well-advanced in the contempt of all cut-people for all those who were not.

'Mind out,' said the bargeman, and began to push forward the beam on which she sat.

'Nanette,' screamed Emma.

Nanette ran to the side of the lock to find, with horror, the boats far beneath her. Their wet sloping cabin-tops dangerously invited her.

'Jump,' cried Charity. 'Quickly Nanette, we're going.' The gates were open, the boats were already moving out.

'I can't, I can't,' said Nanette, dithering miserably sideways and trying to find courage to throw herself down. 'It's too deep, it's too far, I'll break my legs, I can't.'

'Go on,' said the bargeman, grinning, and the lock-keeper shouted out: 'You'll be all right.'

So she jumped, very desperately, her sou'wester blowing from her head in a gust of rain at the same moment.

'My hat, my hat,' she cried, landing with her legs unbroken. 'Charity, quick. . . .'

The sou'wester skidded along the side of the *Ariadne* and flopped heavily into her boiling wake.

'Never mind,' said Emma impatiently from the adjoining deck. 'You can buy another, they're easy enough to get.'

'But that was a special one; it was given to me. It belonged to a man in the Merchant Navy. . . .'

In any case it was too late by this time. The boats were out of that lock and half the distance to the next. Emma was hardhearted about the loss and Charity explained to Nanette the way to jump.

'You *must* land with your knees bent, Nanette. If you keep them stiff like that of course you'll break them, and think how it hurts.'

'Yes, it did,' said Nanette gloomily.

The first three pairs of London locks were so close together that boats, as a general rule, stayed tied abreast. Once clear of the third lock, the *Venus* and the *Ariadne* singled out, and Charity took charge of the steering. Nanette and Emma sat opposite each other in the butty hatches and relaxed.

'I'm sorry about your sou'wester, Nanette. If you like you can borrow my beret.'

'Well, thank you very much, Emma, but it really doesn't matter; I think I look rather nice with wet hair after all.'

We were just then tearing as fast as possible round a bend, Charity noisily blowing on her horn in warning. Immediately round the bend was a bridge-hole. Half-way through this was a barge, and into the barge, unavoidably, we crashed. Several mugs fell from their pegs in the cabin and the kettle rolled on to the floor, making it wetter than it had been.

'Didn't you hear me crack my whip?' yelled the bargeman.

'No, I'm sorry,' shouted Charity, backing away. 'The horn was making such a noise I couldn't hear anything else.'

'Well, lucky you wasn't loaded my girl, else you'd 'a bin sunk by this time.'

He seemed to take the crash good-naturedly. It was possibly not a new experience: at this time there were about twelve girls such as us fooling about with equally unfledged inaptitude up and down the length of the cut. Considering what a nuisance we must have been, they were surprisingly gentle with us and seldom grew angry. The *Venus* bore a dint in her bows from that encounter, the first of a good many more, but the barge was unscratched, for the *Venus*, empty, was light as a pea, and the barge as strong as a battleship.

Charity looked humbly at us and said she might enjoy a cup of cocoa.

Buildings rose, tall, on either side, their dirty stones going deep down into the water, their roof-tops lost far up in the town's grime. Offices, factories or ware-houses – they looked for the most part much the same, and a vague sombre character they had, mere mouldering screens to shut away the busy traffic of the canal from other human contact.

26

Sometimes we saw heads bent, silent over silent work, and the faces they raised to us, white and strange, might have been the faces of prisoners whose pardon had been forgotten. Sometimes they ran to a window, and we saw their mouths cry greetings that our ears could never hear. We waved to them lustily, beaten red with wind and rain. Once a man in dungarees, leaning on the rail of a stairway high up, called out to us, and his voice floated down as though he was at the bottom of a well and the well, in some way, reversed.

Nanette's bargeman was right when he said there was no chance of the weather changing. Rain fell, either as a downpour, or alternatively as a drowning mist, for four consecutive days and at night for certainly as long as we were awake to hear it. But by twelve o'clock that day we were so used to rain dripping from the ends of our noses, from the sleeves of our oilskins, from loose strands of hair, so used to sodden ropes and soaking boots, that we hardly noticed it was raining and had quite ceased to care. The most disagreeable part of it was the wetness of the cabins; for the hatches being necessarily open for steering, rain fell inside and lay in puddles on the stove, the floor and the sidebed, cancelling out the charm of home and comfort that these little match-box houses usually had.

We came to the tunnel that runs beneath the Angel, Islington. And here we had to lie and wait, for a tug was on its way through with a string of barges. Our own boats were narrow enough to pass one another inside the tunnel, but barges were too wide, filling it from side to side, to allow the passage of any other craft. Bargemen, who had had to lead their horses over the top, arrived and stood waiting for their charges on the towpath. And presently another pair of empty boats came up and moored to the opposite bank of the cut, waiting like us.

The tug, with its attendant barges, six of them, floating behind, came very slowly throbbing out of the dark hole, leaving a thick tubeful of yellow smoke to smart our eyes and choke our throats.

As soon as the last barge was gone, Charity tossed aboard the rope that had tied us to shore and Emma set the bows of the *Venus* towards the tunnel. The steerer of the other pair of boats did the same thing at exactly the same moment; the boats raced forward, their bows converging and smacking into one another at the very entrance. Emma, alarmed but determined, kept her finger on the accelerator.

'Get out of my bloody way,' roared the boater.

'No I won't,' shouted Emma, fired to defiance for the first time. 'I was before you – get out of mine.'

'Get out of our bloody way,' cried Nanette, nearly clapping her hands.

It was the birth of pugnacity. And almost certainly the esteem of the boating world for us dated from that moment. The boater dropped astern without another word. We bolted through the tunnel like devils on horseback, more than a little frightened at ourselves, but our hearts rocking with triumph. We thought that this boater, whose name was Sam Stevens, would surely kill or maim us later. Later, however, he became one of our closest friends, championing us with faithful pride on every occasion, mending our engine whenever he happened to find us broken down, and helping forward our career with many crafty tips.

It was in the following pound that we had our first engagement with a new enemy. This enemy was children – little girls as well as little boys – and the method of attack was twofold. Charity was steering the motor at the time. Ahead of us, leaning over the parapet of a bridge, we saw two little boys, apparently, after the manner of little boys, pleasantly occupied in watching boats.

'Hullo,' we called out. They were mute.

Then, just as we passed beneath them, a large blob of spittle struck the cabin-top beside Charity's elbow; a second, more thoughtfully aimed, fell slimily on Nanette's shoulder and mingled with the raindrops. The children burst into shrill cat-calls, sprang away from the bridge and raced down to the towpath where they were joined by a number of other brats. Here they demonstrated the second method of warfare, which took the form of stones, bricks, lumps of dung and any other rubbish that came to hand. We could neither hide nor defend ourselves; we were helpless, and sick with rage. The stones thumped against the sides of the boats, splashed round us in the water and occasionally actually hit us. The more we shouted, and we shouted fearfully, the more they danced and hooted with pleasure.

'Gipsies,' they yelled. 'Dirty gipsies.'

Then a stone struck Charity on the side of her cheek. Had it been a brick she might presumably have died. She went white. Her mild and beautiful eyes blazed with sudden passionate hate. She drove the *Venus* headlong towards the bank, crammed the tiller into Nanette's hand, snatched up a windlass, and, with a leap that was nearly superhuman, reached the bank. The children fled up the tow-path on to the London road. Charity flew after them, her deadly windlass raised in the air, and so they all disappeared.

Sam Stevens came up with us just as we were taking the next lock, and put his boats into the twin lock which was also lying ready. The four boats sank down together. Sam came across, as we waited for the water to empty away, and said:

'Is this yourn?' He was holding out Nanette's sou'wester.

'Oh, thank you,' cried Nanette glowingly. 'It's mine – how good of you.'

Being faster with paddles and gates than we were, he, his family, and his boats, got away ahead of us legitimately enough. Charity jumped aboard just as we were leaving. The scratch on her cheek was still oozing blood.

'I caught one,' she said, 'and a policeman saw me smack him. I told him the reason, and then he understood and let me finish.'

'Did you beat him with the windlass?' asked Nanette.

'No. I think it would have killed him.'

'I would have killed him,' said Nanette.

'He was the smallest,' said Charity.

We were very hungry by the time we reached the last lock. All we wanted was to tie the boats up anywhere and find ourselves some dinner. The lock-keeper looked at our loading order.

'D. Wharf,' he said, pointing over to the left.

The last huge wooden gates swung royally outwards. The pool – so vast it seemed, so spacious and teeming and glamourous – lay open before us like a new world. It was like a birth, it was like the release of doves from a cage, it was like Arctic explorers breaking their ship free after months of ice to find an ocean. We were awed, not only then but every time, by this entrance into freedom after the rigid confinement of the cut. The feeling of newness and discovery was strong.

> '. . . We were the first that ever burst
> Into that silent sea . . .'

It was the lunch hour. The cranes were still. There was no shouting. No chug of engines except what came from our own. Sam Stevens had already made fast and was down below having his dinner. It was as though we were inheritors of a deserted pool. Two merchantmen, which the open sea with its mountainous waves and valleys would dwarf to the size of tin cans, now rose towering above their flat brethren of lighters and barges, and our own boats that seemed suddenly like toys for children to handle. One was lying ready to be unloaded; the other was coaling-up. Close against D. Wharf, to which we now made our way, and lifting its pretty rigging elegantly free from the surrounds of steel and coal and rust, lay a coastal barge, its red sails tight-furled.

'What a pity we can't go to sea,' said Charity.

But dinner was what we chiefly wanted then. With careless speed we tied the *Ariadne* to a lighter; with dangerous haste we scrambled up the vertical iron ladder on to the wharf-side and rushed helter-skelter off to Joe's Dining-Rooms.

The noise and the smoke that greeted us on pushing open the door was stunning. Little light at any time penetrated that small room. Now, with steam and the smoke of innumerable Woodbines clouding its dark corners, it was like stepping into a noisy cave. The whitish neckerchiefs of dockers, packed so closely together that the backs of those sitting at one bench rubbed the backs of those at the next, shone smearily out of the gloom. Some of the men who had finished their dinners, shoved themselves up and out, and we squeezed round the end of a table and studied the black-board:

'Liver and chips.'

'Sausage & mash & bacon.'

'Cottage pie.'

We chose the liver and chips and ordered with it inch-thick slices of bread and butter, after which we champed our way through a pudding and jam, and finished the meal with cups of very strong over-sugared tea.

While we ate, the door behind us banged ceaselessly open and shut. An unseen wireless, turned to its loudest, gave us the entertainment of a rhumba band, and through an open kitchen door came the mad clatter of dishes. Joe himself dived to and fro with slopping tea and loads of food. A cat crept between our feet, searching for scraps or caresses. Knives and forks rattled amongst the hubbub of hoarse voices. The smell was wonderful; the noise was excruciating; the smoke was nearly solid. It was like a hell or a heaven, or a very nice mixture of the two. As for us, we could at that time think of nothing more attractive.

We came back to the docks swollen underneath our jerseys and ready for almost anything.

'You won't get done to-day, girls,' said the foreman, Herbert. We looked at one another.

'Can we go off then?' Quite suddenly the rain, still teeming down, was something from which escape would be a pleasure.

'Well, I don't know about that,' said Herbert. 'They've got some stuff on F. Wharf – they might want to do you there. Better hang around a bit and see.'

So we hung around and watched while Sam Stevens' boats were loaded down with snaky-thin steel billets, bending in mid-air like rods of willow. Presently, tiring of this, we drifted apart. Charity went off to buy provisions and Nanette trundled away to find the Thames. She found it at full tide, seething with the race of hidden currents, blown by the rainy wind into stormy yellow crests, so impelling and energetic, so romantically resourceful in the various craft that fought their way downstream or bucketed up, so wild in the smoky tangles that passing tugs cast upon the air, that she was moved by real excitement and threw her arms above her head and hollered as though she was mad.

Like Charity, she longed to go to sea. She saw herself battling her way across the rough Atlantic, drenched and tossed, and afterwards being congratulated by everyone she knew. Still dreaming of her modest answers, she returned to D. Wharf, and there found Charity, her feet surrounded by string bags and cabbages, gazing down with dismay at the *Ariadne*. The *Venus* was missing.

'Over at F. Wharf,' said Herbert.

They strained their eyes to penetrate the downpour. There on the far side of the pool was the *Venus* in the middle of being loaded. Together they hurried round the dockside, past the piles of rusty steel and pig-iron, past cranes and gangs of men, picking their way over chains, and rope as thick as a leg, till they reached F. Wharf and knelt on the stone to call down to Emma:

'So sorry – did you manage all right?'

'Oh yes, it was really quite easy,' Emma shouted back, standing on the cabin-top in a boastful attitude, her legs apart.

'They only wanted the *Venus*, and they aren't filling her up properly; there was just a bit of steel left, and they wanted to clear it.'

'Shall we come down?'

'Yes, if you like. But there's no need.'

However, down they went and watched the last few billets being swung inboard. Then back across the pool to the *Ariadne*, moving more slowly now, for the *Venus* was partly loaded and a foot or so deeper in the water. Herbert came down to us for a cup of tea and told us about the captain of the coastal barge and his red-haired son of fifteen, who worked as mate to his father.

'Them two,' said Herbert, 'run that little boat of theirs over to Dunkirk and back six or seven times. Don't know how many men they didn't bring back. And when it was all over, old Wally said to his nipper, "Walter," he says – the little chap's called Walter too – "how about running over to-night and having a look round? I've got a feeling," he says, "there's maybe some more we ain't found yet." So they slipped across that night, and there in the dark, sitting out on a bit of rock, they found four of our boys. Course it was all quiet then, the fighting was over and the Jerries were there. Wally had to keep his engine shut. Must have been a funny thing, those boys still hoping someone would find 'em, and Wally having a feeling he ought to go. Nice little place you got in here,' he added.

We were sitting inside the cabin of the *Ariadne* and the stove was red-hot. The hatches were closed, so that all we knew of the rain was the sound it made falling on the roof.

'My dad was a doctor,' said Herbert. 'He lost all his money on the horses. I might have been a doctor myself if he'd 'a gone steady. I'm fifty-five next week,' he said, 'and I don't drink nor smoke nor bet. Nor I didn't ever get married. My dad was a terrible drinker.'

He seemed to us a thoughtful sombre old man, sitting hunched in his steaming overcoat, and we guessed he had a deep religious strain in him to keep him so resigned and sad. Presently he said: 'You girls ought to get married. This ain't no life for you.'

We offered him bread and jam and he shook his head.

'We want to go to sea,' said Charity. 'Do you think they'd take us aboard one of these merchant ships?'

'They do in Russia,' said Nanette.

'We can splice ropes and we're very strong,' said Charity.

'And what do you think those chaps 'ud do to you once they got to sea, eh?' said Herbert.

We hung our heads.

'Oh, I don't *think* so,' said Emma vigorously. 'As Charity says, we're very strong, and there'd be three of us.'

'Yus. And there'd be about twenty chaps, my girl, and things is different at sea, things is rougher, chaps are different. It's no place for a woman. What would your mothers say, eh?'

'Oh, they don't mind what we do,' said Emma.

'My mother's dead already,' said Nanette.

'It wouldn't be right. Ladies ought to stay ashore. Well, I'm obliged to you for the cup of tea. You can go home if you like,' he added, on his way out of the cabin. 'We won't load you any more to-day.'

We washed our faces and washed our hands, and Nanette put on her ear-rings. We padlocked the cabins and threw tarpaulins over the billets in the *Venus* to keep her hold from filling with rain overnight. We clambered up the ladder with a change of clothing in kitbags across our shoulders.

'Eight o'clock in the morning,' shouted Herbert. 'Mind you're here.'

The loaders paused to whistle and yell:

'How about if I come too?'

'Thought you and me was going to the Troxy to-night.'

Down poured the rain. Off we swaggered, wet-footed, cold-fingered, and utterly content with everything about our silly young self-infatuated selves.

34

4

The policeman at the gate was just frying himself an egg and bacon for breakfast. To Emma, who had risen at six and travelled from Hampstead in a cheerless Underground train, the smell was particularly good. She stopped and put her head inside his box.

'Hullo,' he said, lifting a rasher out of the sizzling pan and reversing it. With his helmet lying on the table beside him and the stove between his sprawling knees, he had a domestic unpolicemanlike appearance.

'That looks all right,' she said. He smacked his lips and winked.

'Nice day you brought with you,' he said. 'Come in out of the rain and have a cup of tea.'

'No, thank you very much but I can't. They're going to start loading us at eight. Have the other girls arrived?'

'Not yet. You're the first.'

She climbed down the dripping ladder and unlocked the cabin of the *Ariadne*. It was cold and smelt of damp. Sam Stevens had clothed-up his boats the evening before and was now lying outside the lock-gates waiting for them to be opened. On the far side of the docks were two other pairs of boats, their chimneys smoking. A seaman in a striped jersey and a sweatcap leaned over the rail of a merchant ship, looking sleepily down. Otherwise the docks seemed deserted.

Almost immediately Charity arrived; she was carrying a kitten.

'Charity – a *cat*?'

'Yes, I know – it's a stray. I found it in Gloucester Road station. They said it had been there for days and was sure to be killed by a train if it stayed, so I brought it along with me. It's pretty, don't you think?'

'I wouldn't say it was pretty exactly. It looks rather bitten. And rather fierce too.'

'That's because it's hungry. I'll give it some tinned milk.'

'Not now, Charity. Put it in the cabin. We must have the boats ready by eight o'clock.'

Together we stripped off the tarpaulin sheets, emptying the pools of rain-water over the side.

'Did you have a nice time?'

'Yes I did; I had a huge meal and then a huge bath, and then I went to bed.'

We worked in a half-hearted fashion: memories of comfort were still so close. The loaders came strolling up by ones and twos, and stood on the wharf-side above us, lighting cigarettes and grumbling good-naturedly. At exactly eight o'clock Herbert arrived.

'You ready?' he shouted.

We threw the last planks and stands on to a neighbouring lighter to clear the hold, and said we were. Three of the loaders clambered down aboard the *Venus*; Herbert got out his notebook; the crane-driver began leisurely to mount the various flights of ladder to his little cage high above our heads. Other cranes were starting awake with grunts and whinings. The docks motor-launch was cavorting round the pool like an agitated water-beetle. People were beginning to shout. And on numerous coal-barges old men were laboriously, slowly, working their hand pumps up and down, up and down; humped and shabby, and apparently unpressed by time, apparently unambitious for anything beyond the dismal stream of water they sucked up from under the dirty cargo, apparently tireless, they worked their old arms up and down, up and down, as though their lives had been spent monotonously pumping, and as though, still pumping, they must presently die.

Emma, glancing up, saw Nanette standing on the wharf-side talking to Herbert.

'I went to a lovely party,' shouted Nanette, waving her hand. 'I'm sorry I'm late.'

Then she climbed up the miniature Eiffel Tower to visit the crane-man in his glass-sided box. From here she could see the whole docks at work in a mist of rain, and away beyond the docks, closely hemming in the pool so that it shrank to a puddle, shining rows of roof-tops, factory-chimneys, a hint of the river, the span of a bridge.

'What a wonderful view,' she said to the crane-driver, and he smiled, not hearing her.

Charity was inside lighting the fire. Emma, with a vague idea of supervising the loading, sat cross-legged on the cabin-top in the rain. Her face wore an expression of steady concern. She was not sure if she ought to be giving directions, or complaining in any way. Perhaps if she sat in silence they would despise her and be careless in their loading. However, knowing no better, she remained silent and worried, and the loading seemed to go ahead well enough.

The crane-cable swung inland. A team of men fastened the chains around a bundle of billets and motioned upwards to Bill, the crane-driver, who lifted his load six feet and then swung it out clear of the wharf. Here for a moment it hung in the air, heavily revolving, and then with a sudden rush descended almost upon the *Venus*. At once the three men in the hold began to shout and push and wave their arms.

'Up a bit Bill; over now, bit further; all right, careful now, down a bit.'

The rusty billets, embraced at either end by burly arms to keep them steady and lying straight with the *Venus*, were then lowered by Bill another three feet.

'O.K. Bill, drop her; drop her there, son.'

And the load of steel, landing precisely, set the little *Venus* reeling, like a mailed hand clapped down on a girlish shoulder.

The loaders unhooked the circling chains and stood back. 'All right Bill.'

The chains dragged themselves noisily free of the billets and swung up into the air, twisting and kicking like furious snakes, and Emma ducked in obedience to the warning shouts.

'You want to watch out for those,' said one of the men, crossing his arms and spitting over the side of the boat. 'Get in the way of one of them chains and you'll have your head took off before you know where you are.' He had a finger missing from his left hand and most of the nails were squashed horribly into the flesh.

Between loads they told Emma their habits and hobbies, their ages, the names of their children and their varying opinions about the war. The only way to win it was explained to her and the Government policy corrected. They asked her why she was not married, and other questions about her private life. Emma answered them all. Presently they mentioned tea at the tops of their voices, and Charity appeared at once, burdened with mugs, and much distressed that they should have thought her capable of forgetting so obvious a need. The loaders above clamoured for the same favour. Bill leaned out from his cage and shouted:

'How about me?'

Charity disappeared below in a fluster, and loading was suspended.

'I can't understand,' said Emma, 'how Bill, all that long way up, can hear what you say.'

'Oh, he can't,' said one of the loaders. 'Can't hear a word, he can't. He's much too far off. But he knows. He's been a-doing this job for so long, he knows what we want him to do, he knows by instink. And he ain't never wrong.'

'Then why do you bother to shout to him?'

'Habit,' said the loader.

Every so often the ropes that bound the two boats together had to be loosened, for with each additional weight the *Venus* sank down lower than the still empty *Ariadne*. Charity ran up to the bows to slacken the ropes there, slipped, and fell in. The crane hung still for a moment and in the pause we heard her voice, choked with water, calling for help. She was not, luckily, wearing gum-boots, which would have filled and dragged her down, but her oilskin prevented her from swimming and frightened her with its weight.

''Ullo, sounds like someone's fallen in,' said one of the loaders, leaning over to see who it was.

But while he was wondering, his mate leapt up to the for'ard deck and threw down the end of a rope to anxious Charity. She clutched it, and by this means he drew her round to the side of the *Venus*, where several arms hauled her roughly inboard.

'All right, girl?' shouted down Herbert.

She nodded, spitting and coughing. Emma rushed her away to change. Already her teeth were chattering and her cheeks blue. Nanette came and sat in the hatches while she rubbed herself over with a towel.

'They say,' said Nanette, 'that the pool's bottomless, no one knows how deep it goes. And they say there's a superstition that anyone who falls into the docks gets some kind of disease and has to go to hospital. Do you think it's true? I don't see why it shouldn't be. Anyway, we'll soon know.'

'Rubbish,' said Emma sharply. 'They were pulling your leg. Don't be such a goose, Nanette – you believe everything.'

Charity, feeling pleasantly delicate, locked her fingers round a mug of hot tea. 'What shall we call the kitten?' she said.

At that moment the boat lurched violently to one side and then the other, and Charity's dry pair of trousers were given a shower of scalding tea. They had begun to load the *Ariadne*.

By eleven o'clock both boats were finished. Two other pairs of boats had arrived during the morning, and one of these they began, the moment we were out of the way, to load. We took the *Venus* and *Ariadne* just as they were across the pool to a quiet patch of water near the locks, and here we tied them up to coalbarges and prepared to start the long and tiresome business of clothing-up. Charity, insisting she was quite recovered, emerged to help us.

First the holds, which had bulged open with the weight of cargo, had to be drawn as tightly in as possible by means of chains. These chains extended across each hold from one side to the other, and were screwed together in the middle. Horizontally above these chains were fitted the sturdy little cross-beams, and into slits in the cross-beams were slid the ten-foot stands, posted vertically down the centre of the hold and wedged to keep them steady. On the slender heads of these stands were laid the top-planks, bolted one to another, and forming the path that led from stern to bows of each boat – an airy and quivering path which at first we ventured timidly along like tight-rope walkers, but on which we soon learnt to run at full speed with long bouncing steps. For additional firmness, the top-planks were lashed down with rope to the cross-beams. The skeleton was then complete and ready to have a tarpaulin skin stretched over its bones.

It had, in fact, two over-lapping skins: the side-cloths, which were fixtures that remained rolled tightly up along the gunwales when the boats were empty, and the top-cloths, great loose sheets of tarpaulin that were folded up and stowed away when not in use.

First we unrolled the side-cloths. These were stretched upward and numerous strings, fastened over the top-planks, held them tautly, covering half of the gap between planks and

40

gunwale. Emma and Charity shuffled on their knees along the top-planks, pulling tight and knotting the strings that Nanette, standing more discreetly below in the hold, threaded and handed up to us. Were these strings to break as we tugged at them, we should be plunged either into the hold, or overboard into the water. It was for this reason we examined them often during each trip, splicing on new ones wherever there appeared to be a weakness. They were coarse and hairy, very harsh on the hands, and before long our old blisters had blossomed out anew and fresh ones were threatening.

Then we shook out the unwieldy top-cloths and spread them as an over-coat covering altogether top-planks, side-strings and side-cloths. These too were fastened down with strings. More blisters broke the surface. Again we shuffled from one end of the boat to the other, Nanette still serving us from beneath. This done, the *Venus* was finished; her hold was completely covered, her cargo hidden out of sight, and she herself had taken on a suave well-dressed appearance. With burning fingers and creaking backs we turned to the *Ariadne*.

'Charity, have you got the big spanner?'

'No, I haven't, I left it on the cabin-top. Can I borrow the hammer a moment?'

'Here you are – catch.'

'No, no, don't – don't throw it; I shall drop it in. Wait – I'll fetch it.'

'Emma, don't pull so *suddenly*.'

'Well, move a bit faster, Nanette.'

And five minutes later: 'Nanette, for God's sake – this isn't the time to wave to sailors.'

However, Emma was wrong. The particular seaman to whom Nanette had waved at once deserted his lofty perch aboard the *Marie-Louise* and came down to us bringing a friend. With their assistance we clothed the *Ariadne* up in half the time.

Nanette was triumphant, and hissed in Emma's ear: 'There, you see.'

We invited them to stay for dinner.

'We don't mind,' they said, and ate a good deal of our stew.

Because they went to sea, where we were forbidden to follow, we found them romantic, and one of them, in addition, had long curling black lashes. They were both about eighteen, or possibly younger. They wore stocking caps and about their jersies clung a pleasant sea-ish manly smell. One of them came from Birmingham and this, being our own destination, brought us closer together. Nanette promised to visit his mother as soon as we arrived. With little to say, they were nevertheless reluctant to leave us. Round them hung a certain dumb wistfulness, asking for more than love.

After we had started up the engine and were lying waiting outside the lock for the gates to open, the Birmingham one came running back. He knelt on the stone and dropped down to us a packet of sugar, a tin of jam, and a paper-bag of figs.

'We got lots of food,' he said.

Nanette, however, never went to see his mother; she lost the address.

There was any amount of traffic that afternoon. Our progress was slow. Now that the boats were loaded, the butty was forever separated from the motor. There was no question of running up to the bows of the *Ariadne* with a mug of tea, and dropping down on to the deck of the *Venus*, as was the comfortable custom with empty boats. We towed the *Ariadne* up the London locks on a short strap in order to keep her well to heel.

There were three methods of towing the butty. One was with the snubber, a thick seventy-five-foot rope used only in long pounds, and running between the stern of the motor-boat and the bows of the butty. One was with a strap, a smaller edition of the snubber, varying from ten yards to two, and used in short and winding pounds. And the third was much more complicated, seldom used by us, and never by families where there were small children aboard.

In this last case the rope was passed all along the top-planks, through running-blocks, and finally through a pulley hanging to one side of the mast. The mast being nearly amidships, the butty in consequence took an indirect pull and could run more freely from side to side, or whither she would. Coiled yard upon yard in the butty hatches was the bulk of the rope, and it was for the butty-steerer to let out as much or as little as she wanted, checking it when the distance between the two boats suited her fancy. Its advantage lay in taking the strain gradually, and so surviving longer than the straps that existed from jerk to jerk till the last jerk broke them. But it was a nuisance for the butty-steerer who had enough on her hands in any case, and could also be dangerous, entangling arms or legs as it ran out.

The manner of taking a pair of boats into a lock was an art which no amount of practice on our part ever made quite perfect. The motor was taken into the right-hand side of the lock and the bows aimed to bump the wall very gently about half way up. The moment the bows bumped, the motor-boat was braked by the engine being put into reverse gear, continuing then to grope her way into the lock, as a blind man feels his way, the stern automatically swinging over to lie flush with the wall. The steerer had, in the meantime, bent to unhook the strap from the motor-deck, coil it and throw it aboard the bows of the butty which duly slid into the lock on the left alongside the motor. At this moment the motor-boat knocked her nose against the sill at the far end of the lock – softly, if her speed had been accurately judged, or, if it had not, with a solid thump – whereupon the steerer whipped her engine into neutral, sprang to the cabin-top, from there leapt up on to the lock-side and ran back to close the gate behind her.

The butty-boat steerer was going through a more harassing experience, for she had no engine with which to brake her boat. The butty, given weigh by the motor-boat and now

43

abandoned, was rushing into place at a fearful speed, and unless checked immediately would crash against the far end, smashing the china in the cabin, spilling the water, and doing indescribable damage to herself. So as soon as the bows had begun to enter the lock, the steerer lifted the heavy wooden tiller clear out from the helm and stood it in the hatches. Next she picked up a length of rope, the other end of which was attached to the side of the butty, and with this in her hand and her windlass in her belt, flung herself on to the steps as the boat swept by them. The steps were taken two at a time in order to gain advantage on the butty, and the rope twirled three times round the nearest bollard. Thus the butty was gently arrested, and after arrest the rope was unwound, carried forward to the next bollard and here tied firmly. No amount of agitation excused the last part of the operation. For the butty, if left untied, drifted backwards; the wooden helm wedged itself beneath a beam of the gate; the water rose, the bows of the boat rose with it, the helm remained pressed down, and the boat sank.

That we seldom brought ourselves through a lock exactly according to rule, it is unnecessary to add – we took the boats in too fast or too slowly, we bumped the wall in the wrong place or not at all, we tied the butty loosely or left the motor-boat in gear when she should have been in neutral, or erred in one of a dozen other ways each time.

But the London locks were well staffed with energetic keepers who, in the kindest possible manner, shut our gates for us, wound our paddles and generally shepherded us through with fatherly concern. It was in the country, when there was perhaps one keeper in five miles, and he old and his bicycle hardly younger – then it was that the onus of locks, the filling and emptying, the entering and leaving of them, fell upon us. The London locks were built in pairs, traffic being heavy. But the country locks lay singly, for barges outside London were less frequent, becoming more rare with every northward mile, and stopping altogether short at Tring Summit.

It was a pleasant afternoon. We dawdled on our way in the best of spirits. There was much to see and many people to talk to and the minutes were crowded.

'You got a good set of teef, girl,' said one old fellow, who was sitting warming himself over a fire in a lock-side hut.

A little confused, Emma replied: 'Yours are nice too.'

They were certainly browner than hers and he had fewer, but considering his age they did him credit.

'Ah,' he said, 'I know how to keep 'em. I rub 'em over wiv me finger night and morning. Cold water and a good rub, that's what does it.' He opened his mouth to show the hidden ones at the back, and she respectfully bent her head to peep inside.

Charity admired the kitchen garden of one lock-keeper, and he at once tore up a handful of leeks and gave them to her as a present. She, in gratitude, dived below and brought out the kitten to show him. He happened to have a special liking for cats, and he and Charity became friends for as long as she was on the cut.

'It hasn't got a name yet,' she said.

'Call it Elsie,' he said. 'My wife's called Elsie.'

The faces of two large orange cats stared at us from a window of his house as we left the lock. His wife we never saw, and we called the kitten not Elsie but Cleopatra.

We passed between the quiet wet green banks of Regent's Park, and tied for the night at Paddington. It was early when we stopped the engine, but our day had been a long one and we were too tired to feel guilty. Rain still fell in gentle whispering abundance. We fried ourselves sausages for supper, and ate them yawning.

It was after supper, when bed seemed to be the next pleasure, that Charity, who had gone outside to fill the kettle, leaned her head into the butty cabin and said:

45

'Emma, there's a man waving to me.'

'He must think you're Nanette,' said Emma sourly.

'No, he's a stranger,' said Charity, her hair falling forward in two dark curtains round her earnest face. 'He's up in a house, waving. He's waving a bottle.'

Out we hastened. We had tied the boats to railings. Immediately beyond the railings was a road, and beyond the road rose decorous plaster-fronted houses. A street lamp shone dimly across the tow-path on to our boats. We crowded together in the hatches of the *Ariadne*, staring up at a brightly-lit open window on the first floor of one of these houses. Though not yet fully dark it was certainly past the black-out time and the window was startling, a positive beacon. Leaning out of it was a young man, who, seeing three of us instead of one, again waved his bottle and called:

'Come up and have a drink.'

'He's in his dressing-gown,' said Charity in a low voice.

At that moment a girl in a red dress leaned across his shoulder and looked out at us curiously. We continued to stare, uncertain of what to do, or how to answer.

'Look,' said Nanette, whispering, 'a Negro.'

A dark face had appeared behind the other two. We turned to one another in the rain, questioning. Experience was obviously beckoning to us from a window. So, with sudden courage, we shouted up our acceptance, at which the young man immediately drew the curtains and left us to enjoy our cold feet in the gathering gloom. Nervous again, we decided we ought to go armed. But windlasses were too bulky. Our knives were too blunt.

'I've got a razor-blade,' said Nanette.

We rubbed our young throats with keen discomfort. In the end we approached two part-time policemen and explained the position.

'It's a bad district,' they said.

'We must go *now*,' said Emma. 'We said we would.'

46

'I wouldn't advise it,' said one of the policemen, shaking his head. 'Don't know what you're letting yourselves in for.'

'Tell you what,' said the other, 'we'll keep an eye on the house, and if you aren't down in half an hour we'll knock on the door.'

'And if no one answers, you must break it down,' said Nanette.

They promised to do this for us.

The girl in the red dress let us in and told us her name was Rachel. A perambulator stood in the hall, and seeing this our fears subsided. The Negro was a professional singer with excellent though shy manners, and sat all evening at a piano singing quietly to himself. Rachel, who was a candid girl not very much older than ourselves, told us she earned a living whenever she could by decorating the walls of cafés. She showed us a number of her canvases which we found different indeed from our postcards in the *Ariadne*. Anxious to be polite, we studied them in silence. The young man in a dressing-gown was her husband, on leave from the army. During the two hours we stayed he drank continuously, walking with extreme agitation up and down the big untidy room, his face becoming whiter and more worried with every minute. Rachel kept her eyes on him while she was talking to us.

'Don't drink any more, Nicky,' she said to him several times, very gently. He took no notice of this remark except once, when he kissed her affectionately. We bunched ourselves together, understanding nothing but feeling vaguely distressed and in the way.

'I often see you going up and down the canal,' said Rachel. 'Well, not you perhaps, but boats like yours. They look so gay. I often think: "How nice to live in one".'

She cooked us a large omelette and we ate it gratefully, not mentioning our previous supper.

Nicky took us into the next room and woke up his daughter,

47

who was four months old. He sat her on the mantelpiece, where her head rolled from side to side.

'She's called Melissa,' said Nicky with great tenderness. He tried to put a flower behind her ear and stuck it in her eye instead. Melissa cried and cried with all her power.

'Oh Nicky,' said Rachel, standing in the doorway. 'She was asleep.'

The Negro had stopped singing and was sitting still in front of the piano, listening.

As far as the part-time policemen were concerned, we might have been slaughtered; they made no attempt to rescue us and had evidently forgotten our understanding. Or perhaps, since it was a bad district, they were rescuing someone else.

5

The alarm clock went off at six, and Emma, knowing that the alternative to immediate response was no response at all for at least another hour, rolled herself out of bed and reached down for the Primus.

She and Charity had arranged to take the early rising in weekly shifts. The cabin was very cold and the air she breathed in tasted of damp unhealthily mixed with the staleness of sleep. She poured the methylated spirits round the gutter of the Primus, her newly-awakened mind entirely concentrated on its liquid amethyst. No thought of home disturbed her. She was not even conscious of the day that stretched ahead. The squeak of the cork as she pressed it back, the smell on her fingers, the fumes of the spirits as she set a match to them – these signs engrossed her wholly. That first half-hour was a bleak time of hardly more than semi-existence. Her cast-off blankets had a congealed, distasteful look. The cabin was in a state of cold and slovenly untidiness. The stove was rusty. Only Charity, asleep in the corner, continued to hold a little world of life around her, being unaware of the ashy morning. Across her neck lay Cleopatra, also asleep.

Warmth was the first necessity, and then food, and after that, order. To these ends Emma devoted herself, thoughtless of anything beyond. She bundled into jersies and trousers while the methylated spirits gave off its pretty dying flame, and then carefully pumped at the Primus until it broke into a low roar. This sound was her first companion.

With the kettle heating on top for tea, she turned to the stove, a miniature kitchen range. The dead cinders were raked aside, newspaper was stuffed in, splinters of wood, a covering of coal and a little paraffin poured on to counteract the general dampness. Coal we had in plenty, for in addition to the lumps that passing coal-barges threw us, we laid in a private supply when visiting the coal-fields for cargo. She put a match to the paper, and as it burst into flame, the cabin for the first time took on an air of humanity, seemed a place for habitation. For a fire, whether in a house or a cabin or a hut, is the heart of existence, and without its beating there is a paralysis of life, the stillness and gloom of death. Emma, becoming human, remembered she must brush her teeth and comb her hair. Becoming more human, remembered she must wake Nanette.

Nanette was no easy person to wake. She clung tenaciously to sleep. She resisted, every morning, efforts to tear her from her favourite occupation. Emma had learnt to be rough, and, as time went on, grew rougher. At first she had contented herself with banging on the top of Nanette's cabin, but learning the futility of this, now climbed down inside the cabin and after shaking her by the shoulder and loudly shouting: 'Breakfast – wake up,' stripped the blankets clean off Nanette's closely-curled body.

Charity, with native obedience, took her waking easily. She had learnt to dress herself quietly, without effort, still sitting in her bed. With all of us dressing was a matter of sixty seconds. The three jerseys we each of us wore stayed together, one inside the other, for days or even weeks at a time, and were put on as a single garment. We also wore boots, men's long pants and a variety of caps. Trousers seemed always to be held together with safety-pins for we had neither the time nor the inclination to sew on buttons or mend fastenings.

Breakfast was simple, consisting of tea and a quantity of bread, butter and marmalade. By the time we had finished, the stove was glowing red, hot enough to boil up subsequent kettles, and the Primus was stowed away. Our table was the front of our food cupboard, which let down as a flap. Our milk came out of tins. We ate in silence, except for Charity's remarks to Cleopatra, and the pattering of rain above.

'I wish it would stop raining,' said Nanette at last. 'I'm tired of it. And my bed was soaking wet last night. We'll die of rheumatic fever.'

'I'd forgotten it,' said Emma. 'I don't think it's coming down so hard.'

Forgotten or not, we lingered on in the slummy comfort of the cabin, even allowing ourselves to become a little sleepy again. Charity drew out Cleopatra's tail between her fingers and laid her cheek between the black ears. Emma and Nanette set their elbows amongst the sticky crumbs and smoked away a five-minute luxury of peace.

'Engine,' said Emma, stubbing out her cigarette. It was nearly seven o'clock.

The engine was by now a familiar devil. We accepted its lack of co-operation and saved our tempers. By seven o'clock we had untied the ropes from the railings and were ready to go. A three-hour pound lay ahead of us, and for this long stretch of water the butty was towed on the snubber.

Emma, who was taking the motor for the first hour, started slowly ahead, Charity paying out the heavy inert length of snubber from the small hold in the for'ard deck. When the seventy-five foot had all unwound itself and flopped into the water, the butty gave a jerk, as though recollecting a forgotten duty, and followed obediently behind. The boats, so widely divided, seemed to be separated even farther from one another by the rain driving down between them. To Nanette steering the butty, Emma appeared a remote and insubstantial figure, a lonely exile, altogether out of reach.

51

The hours that one spent in this way on the deck of the *Venus* formed a peculiar part of one's life, a second little life of withdrawal, different from all other hours. One was alone, but not lonely, nor bored, nor wasting time; time, by an odd inversion, was the waster. One did nothing – nothing except inquiringly stare ahead, and move one's hand to one side or the other. The houses, the countryside, floated evenly past, yet one's feet remained still and growing every moment colder. And one's mind, with a queerly mixed detachment, roamed over every field of thought, touched on the old perplexities, worked its way with unhurried thoroughness round new ones, argued through conversations, conjured up faces and tags of poetry, even feasted on single words, breaking them down into letters and individual sounds and so discarding them. And all the time one's eyes flickered ahead searching for approaching traffic, or a difficult bend. Every thought was intermingled with contemporary vision, possessing the freshness of rain, or the despondency of cows clamped together under a tree, the vivid pleasure of travelling sunshine, or the gravity of evening.

Nor did we at any time forget that while we rose and went to bed at whatever hour suited us, struggled and sweated with wet ropes and dirty cargo, ate what we pleased, wore what we fancied, and generally did as we liked, most girls of our age were in uniform and their lives severely ordered. Independence in fact, then out of bounds to so many, was the touchstone of our joy. We exaggerated its outward appearance, travelling on trains like utter ragamuffins, and remaining needlessly dirty when abroad in London or on leave. For we considered we were lucky, and that our sisters and most of our friends, compared to us, led lives of unqualified misery. Rather naturally, our sisters thought the same of us.

Had it not been for the war we should never have known what it was to travel on a canal. Yet war was little more than a distant noise in our ears. We had no wireless; we never read a newspaper; except from time to time, we met only people to whom 'Europe' was a word casually heard, signifying nothing. The boaters, travelling through the heart of England as their fathers and grandfathers and great-grandfathers had done, were a race apart, little known and knowing little beyond their ancient lore. The life was absorbing, and we were absorbed by it, by the daily problems of advancing as far and fast as possible, and the nightly achievement of tying-up.

Nanette steered the butty, and Charity, who was a natural housewife and unable to think of any menial task as drudgery, tidied up the cabin. She black-leaded the stove and swept up the narrow floor and straightened out Emma's mattress and bedding which were left by day lying on the side-bed as a form of sofa. Emma and Nanette were only too thankful to leave such things to Charity, preferring to bale the hold or polish the engine, or do anything, in fact, except housework.

'What shall we have for dinner to-day?' asked Charity, tilting her head to peer up and out at Nanette.

Nanette thought for some time. 'I don't know,' she said at last.

'How about a kedgeree? I could open a tin of salmon and I know we've got some rice somewhere.'

'Make a lot of it. I get so hungry. And let's have a pudding to-day, for a treat. Let's have fried bread and jam. I love jam,' said Nanette. 'I brought back three pots of it.'

A door at the back of the butty-cabin opened directly into the hold. Three feet of the hold had been partitioned off to act as a general store-room. Here the coal and vegetables were kept. Here the oilskins were hung at night, and here were stacked the spare parts and odds and ends of rope. It was from here that Charity now collected the potatoes that she afterwards, sitting on the side-bed, humming, began to peel into a bucket.

At half past eight she relieved Emma on the motor. The only time one could leap ashore was in the narrow neck of a bridge-hole when a boat could be steered close in along the side. In the open cut it was impossible, on account of mud, to come anywhere near the tow-path. Charity, therefore, jumping off at one bridge-hole raced ahead to the next one, and waited there till the *Venus* came alongside. Emma relinquished the tiller and stepped off at the same moment as Charity stepped on, and Nanette presently picked Emma up with the butty.

At ten o'clock we arrived at the depot, feeling as though we had been abroad in wind and weather for a great deal longer than three hours, feeling as though we were making port after a long and perilous journey. Feeling, in fact, a trifle heroic. We turned, not to the left towards the idle lay-by, but to the right, towards Birmingham, and here we tied up for a few minutes to fetch our letters. We left our engine running, intending to be off again almost at once.

'We'll read them later,' said Emma, as we scampered towards the office.

'No,' said Nanette, 'we won't. Five minutes won't make any difference. Let's have a cup of tea in the canteen and read them quickly there. I'm frozen, and I'm wet and I do want a cup of tea.'

So we drank tea and dripped on to the floor of the empty canteen and dripped on to the strange and ordinary news that loving friends and parents had addressed to: 'Boats 504 – *Venus* and *Ariadne*,' till the ink ran together and the words smeared indecipherably, one into another. We scalded our mouths with hurried gulping, for we had no business to have stopped at all. Once loaded, honour and tradition bade us press forward without indulgence.

'Come on, come on,' said Emma.

We tore back to the boats and were just casting off the ropes with guilty haste, when Charity said:

'The bicycles . . . .'

We had forgotten them. We were appalled. Without bicycles we should have been about as helpless as a rowing-boat without oars. They were waiting for us, one belonging to

Emma and the other to Charity, in the oil-shop. One was laid on the cabin-top of the butty, and the spare one stowed away in the hold amongst the steel. And we were off at last, really off. Good-bye to the lay-by, good-bye to London and comfort. Five days of toil and open country lay ahead of us. One hundred and forty-two locks awaited us before we berthed at Birmingham.

Within an hour we were in lock-country and there was no more companionship of two in the butty. The bicycle was dragged from the cabin-top, and mounted on this Nanette flew ahead of us to prepare the way, like a gospel-spreader of old. Evidently there was a pair of boats just in front and going the same way, for to begin with all the locks were against us and had to be reversed.

Arriving at one of these deserted, tree-surrounded country locks, Nanette fell from her bicycle and flung it aside on the path. There was no time to treat a bicycle with kindness; this one, after only a week or two, was in a sad condition with rusty spokes, the front mudguard missing, the back one bent, and sundry pieces of string tying its other loose bits together. At night it lay out on the cabin-top in the rain. Yet, having rapidly reached a certain state of decay, it decayed no further, and as a hard-worked hideous wreck of machinery stayed in service for just over a year, when its front wheel fell off altogether and was lost in the cut.

The lock at which Nanette threw her bicycle down bore the date of 1863, and the rain that splashed her legs as she ran lay in hollows worn into the stone by generations of boaters' boots. The four enormous beams tilting at either end of the lock were graven with the names and initials of sweethearts who were dead, or whose grandchildren now carved new hearts in the old blackish wood. The tall trees, dripping soberly round Nanette as she closed the far gate, must have been upstart youngsters at that time when raw stone and fresh-hewn wood were being fashioned to the shape of a lock.

Immense silence, combining permanence with the present moment's rain, distilled an ancient sweetness. The rattling fall of a paddle released by Nanette, sounded like broken glass in an empty auditorium. Neither the boats approaching nor the boats already gone were within earshot, and even had they been the sound of their engines could have disturbed that peacefulness no more than the tick of a clock across the history of a dream. Slow rot and ageless slime brooded about the lapping water. How ghost-like, how dying and frail, how part of nothing lasting, must have seemed the endless procession through of gay boats and ruddy faces, always passing on with noise and haste, one after the other, year after year.

With no thought of this in her head, only the need pressing on her to have the lock empty and the gates open by the time her boats drew into sight, Nanette slopped her way all round the lock, down one side, across the sloping slippery beams of the shut gates and up the other side to close the other gate. Enormously heavy, it yet swung in the full water lightly to and fro, played upon by every ripple, as loose and easy as an unanchored dinghy. Nanette gave it a last angry push to settle the matter and trotted back to wind the opposite paddles.

Afterwards she leaned over, watching the smooth face of water that lay outside at the foot of the gates. A blossom, a moving flower, broke through the surface like a lily thrusting upwards to unfold, silently and hurriedly, its petals. Another dawned, and then another, and then the water was heaved up in violent confusion and tossed and torn aside by a great escaping flurry, a torrent, a noisy avalanche of white and green. It tumbled and poured out from the open sluices, and at the far end the gates banged heavily together as the level in the lock sank and the water was sucked from them.

Nanette stretched herself at full length along a beam and lay there at her leisure, rain on her face and the odour of old soaking wood in her nostrils. She turned her cheek and found close to her eye a world, enlarged to immensity, of small green mosses, chips and pebbles, a weed or two, stranded and living together in a cleft of the wood with the tranquillity of ignored existence.

The rush of water slackened; she sat up. The lock was almost empty. Outside, the tumult had ceased and only brownish froth and large shining bubbles floated away in breaking, dissolving circles. At the same moment her ear caught the familiar pattering, and round the corner appeared the bows of the *Venus*. Rather gingerly, for this was one of the things she hated and feared to do, she slithered her feet down to the point where the two great gates met one another. Standing on one of them and holding very firmly indeed to the hand-rail, she began with her left foot to press the other gate apart and push it wide open. It moved grandly a few inches; she shoved again desperately, stretching her legs wide, clutching with all her terror to safety. Terrible visions of the slip, the fall, and death by drowning beset her as she poised there, straddled between the two gates, one of them reluctantly moving from her. She kept her foot upon it as long as she dared, encouraged it with a last backward kick, and retreated thankfully to the lockside to push open the second gate. The alternative way of opening gates was to run all round the lock again, and as the day was full of locks and running, a little danger and fright was preferable to greater fatigue.

'I believe the locks are all against us,' called out Nanette as we came into ear-shot. 'There must be a pair of beastly boats just ahead of us.'

However, when she reached the next lock she found a youth already sitting astride one of the beams, laconically picking his nose. A windlass hung round his neck. She bicycled back along the tow-path and waved her arms at the oncoming *Venus* and *Ariadne*. Charity slowed the *Venus* down and stretched out her neck to understand, at which Nanette held up one hand with two of her fingers raised – a sign used on the cut to mean: 'Boats a-coming.' Charity immediately braked the *Venus* by putting her engine into reverse, and Emma steered the butty on to the mud. There they waited while Nanette bicycled happily back to talk to the lock-wheeler.

'How many locks have you made ready for us?' she asked him.

He considered for a moment. 'Three,' he said at length. There was a silence.

'How many you made ready for us?' he finally asked.

'Four,' said Nanette, 'or five – four I think. Four anyway.'

She strove to think of something else to say, and failed. They sat together on the same beam and waited. The boy, she judged, was about sixteen, small, as nearly all the boaters were, with slightly bowed legs. His boots were nailed, his coat collar was turned up, round his waist was tied a piece of string in place of the usual leather belt. He looked, not at Nanette, but away from her indifferently, up the cut. His thick un-touched hair fell forward completely hiding his brows, and almost overhanging his eyes. He tilted his chin up, as though looking out from under the brim of a hat. With a sudden flash of inspiration Nanette sensed that he was not antagonistic, nor unaware of her, but keenly conscious that she sat beside him and that they were foreign, one to another.

He was not in the very least self-conscious. Indeed, lacking any individual personality, he was instead only the fragment of a mass personality. Stripped of all subtlety by simple living and much physical hard work, he was dumb, quite helpless as far as any social expression was concerned, without either the impetus or the impudence of the bargemen, but ready, even expectant, waiting for something to happen. A windlass dropped into the cut, an accident of some kind, a cry for help, would bring them together. She was hesitant of sacrifi-cing a windlass and cast desperately about her for another excuse. The bicycle, a puncture – but already it was too late: his own boats were in sight, were quickly approaching. She was cut off from all possible contact, denied the leap she loved of mind to friendly mind, though there they were, both friendly she knew, and for a few minutes visibly close to one another. She looked at him sadly, as at a lost friend, and he continued not to meet her glance.

Nanette stood back, admiring the smoothness with which these boats glided into the lock, not a bump out of turn. The gates were shut, the paddles drawn, the boats sinking, with an off-handed ease that told of more than one life-time's practice. The woman, a bright-eyed sharp-faced creature who was scrubbing her washing on the back end of the butty hatches, nodded towards Nanette in a kindly way. The husband too, as he lumbered by, seemed to have a sympathetic look in his eye. Again she yearned for the crowning touch, for the bright spark of affection to flash between them. The boy had bicycled slowly on. She said to the woman deceitfully, for she already knew what the answer was:

'How many locks have you made ready for us?'

'Three,' said the woman at once. 'There's a pair of boats right in front of you. But there's more boats a-comin'; you'll have more ready later.'

'Come,' thought Nanette, comforting herself with Alice-like dialogue. 'That's better: she really spoke to me quite a lot. And I do believe she likes me, I really think she does.'

'Isn't it wet?' she shouted, much elated.

'Ah, it's a booger, this weather,' agreed the woman, and to prove beyond doubt her friendly intention, she raised one hand from the wash-tub and nodded as her boat slid away.

Since three locks were ready for us, there was no need of a lock-wheeler. Nanette parked her bicycle on the cabin-top of the *Ariadne* and ate a belated lunch. We had already eaten ours while we steered, our platefuls of kedgeree blown cool by the wind and moistened by falling rain. Nanette bolted hers down, fearful of being disturbed before her hunger was finished.

'It's very good,' she said, peering out at Charity who was labouring at the tiller of the butty, 'how clever you are,

Charity, I could never cook that stuff if I tried for a fort-night.'

'It's quite easy,' said Charity, bending down to reply to this praise. 'I'm sure you could; anyone could.'

The butty, her course undirected for a moment, seized the opportunity of sliding out of line with the *Venus* and ground-ing herself on the mud. Emma angrily shouted. Charity threw her weight on the tiller and rowed like a slave. The *Ariadne* corrected herself.

'We're just coming to a lock,' said Charity. 'I'm so sorry, Nanette – have you had time to finish?'

'Well, I can have my pudding in the next pound,' said Nanette, picking up her windlass with a backward glance at the jam.

The afternoon passed with surprising speed; the hours slid by as unnumbered as the locks we left behind us. Twice we met a pair of boats, and in each case they had made two locks ready and one of us could rest aboard instead of bicycling on.

One pair of boats was on the beer run. Beer, which in actual fact was not beer but Guinness, was a light cargo and so had priority of passage. Anyone, at any time, had to let the beer go by them. Usually these beer-boats – fly-boats they were some-times called – were crewed only by men or boys, for although the pay was good, running the beer was reckoned no kind of family life. The work was incessant, for they were kept to a strict schedule, running all night through the black-out with shaded headlights. Very often three boys would take to the beer for a few months in order to make quick money, and then go back to the comparative peace of ordinary boating. But one family we came to know, the Fosters, kept on the beer run month after month, and, to the best of our knowledge, year after year. The children were always clean, the mother neatly dressed, the boats sparkling with brass and shining with scrubbed wood. They were forever passing and repassing us, always in the most cheerful tempers, seldom tired. The mother was an intensely self-respecting woman, self-proud, children-proud, house-proud, and she must have worked like a great healthy well-fed demon to have kept them as they were.

These boys on the beer-boats who passed us now, nice-looking smartish boys, refused to say a single word. They even indicated the number of locks ready for us by silently holding up their fingers. This was not due altogether either to truculence or shyness: they were all three courting, and terrified in case a hint of infidelity should, with the surprisingly infiltrative powers of cut gossip, reach the ears of their scattered girls. The holds of their boats were piled high with barrels, giving them a top-heavy appearance, for beer was the one cargo over which no time was wasted in clothing-up. They swept by us with almost the same high royal prows as empties, and left us rocking in their wash.

At about four o'clock, when tiredness was beginning to slow our movements, and dampness to clog our feet, we ran into trouble. Charity was ahead lock-wheeling. She came bicycling back to us with great energy, wildly waving her arms. Nanette, on the motor, slowed down.

'What is it?'

'The gate. I can't open one of the gates. There's something jammed behind it.'

'Well, try again. We'll come along slowly.'

Charity disappeared, bent double over the handle-bars. When a few minutes later, barely moving, we rounded the bend and saw the lock ahead of us, one gate was still half-shut and Charity was poking down behind it with the long shaft that lies beside all locks in case of emergency. She shook her head at us despairingly and screamed:

'No good. Can't move it. I don't know what it is.'

She pushed again at the beam, and the gate remained unmoving. The *Venus* and *Ariadne* hung drifting about outside. Presently Charity came down to the tow-path for a consultation.

'Tell you what,' said Nanette. 'I'll run the motor in as fast as I can against the gate and try to bang it open. We can't stay here all day.'

The *Venus* was accelerated to her full capacity and hurled forward, her bows hitting the gate with a fearful thud. The gate groaned and creaked and moved shudderingly open. But the *Venus*, thrown out of her intended path by the onslaught, bounded to one side and lay diagonally across the lock from corner to corner. Emma on the *Ariadne* was powerless to check the butty's following rush. In she tore, buried her nose in the narrow crevasse allowed her by the *Venus*, and so jammed. The *Venus* was tightly wedged between one corner of the lock and the other; the *Ariadne* was tightly wedged between the crooked *Venus* and the wall of the lock. Neither boat would budge an inch.

We tried everything. We tried putting the motor ahead and then whipping her violently into reverse gear. We tried to drag the butty back by hand. We tried to flush the boats out by drawing the farther paddles and letting the water waste through. Nothing moved them. We were stuck. Our morning energy was dead and gone; we were tired and sick and swearing, hating the boats, hating the cut, hating the constant dreary numbing rain.

At this moment, appearing for the second time like an opportune angel, Eli Blossom came bicycling up the tow-path. He seemed delighted to find us in such a situation. He said very little, but grinned like a fool from ear to ear as he walked round looking down at the boats from every angle. At last he said:

'Soon get you out of that.'

It was impossible not to fall in love with him.

His boats appeared, Dad on the motor, Mum Blossom on the butty. Picking up the long shaft, Eli very nimbly pole-vaulted aboard the motor and his Dad retired, for it seemed tacitly understood that this was Eli's moment. He hitched the

Ariadne's stern to the bows of his motor, and in less than two minutes had dragged her backwards free from the jaws of the lock. The *Venus* was pushed across to her rightful side and the blockage was over.

Our spirits revived, and so did our strength. But the Blossoms having helped us once were determined to help us further. For the next eight locks Eli lock-wheeled for both pair of boats, and at seven o'clock we all tied up together like a family party.

Nanette, who had been making fast the bows of the boats, came back to the butty cabin with a glowing face.

'Eli wants me to go to the pictures with him,' she said.

Emma, who had thought that Eli favoured her, was disgusted. 'Well you can't,' she said, 'if you go to the pictures with him it means you're courting.'

'Well, why not?' said Nanette mildly. 'I like Eli.'

'Think what the other boaters would say. Think how the women would hate us. Think of the gossip.'

It was partly true.

'It's awfully late,' said Charity, who took no sides but was practical.

In the end we ate a hurried supper and went off to a pub with the Blossoms instead. Emma and Charity sat in a dark corner and drank beer with Mr. and Mrs. Blossom. Nanette and Eli played darts.

'You can call me anything you like,' said Eli, 'so long as you don't call me late for breakfast.'

He was a lively boy, once he got going, with a turn for wit. Nanette played darts badly, and so, surprisingly, did Eli. The game went on for a long time.

Mrs. Blossom was so fat that two slits had been cut in her black pinafore in order that her bosom might lie outside in comfort, unconfined. She wore an old open-work crotcheted jumper and her arms at all times, winter and summer, indoors and out, even in snow-storms, were bare to above the elbow.

She told us Eli was not, at the moment, courting, though he had once had a girl called Ida.

'They was goin' together two–three years,' she said. 'But one was scared and t'other was frit, so nothin' come of it.' Happily she seemed to approve of Nanette.

The lobes of her ears hung low, almost to her shoulders, with the weight of gold ear-rings. The original holes had been stretched into long trenches, which she had made herself, she said, with a pin. She offered to deal with Emma's ears in the same way, and even began as a proof of earnestness to unfasten a brooch from her jersey. Emma, in secret horror, refused the kindness.

Mr. Blossom, who sat chuckling on the other side of Charity, had a long stiff neck bound so tightly in a white scarf that it seemed to be bandaged in splints. From his left ear dangled a gold ring, like a pirate's. He sat on his bench very upright, swilling back his beer, wiping his mouth over and over again, and telling Charity stories of the cut without looking at her, staring in front of him, chuckling.

When we had stumbled back to the boats through rain and darkness, he nudged Charity in the ribs, and then, holding aloft a hurricane lamp in one hand, tried to execute a smart little dance along the top-plank of their motor-boat. Being unsteady on his feet he slipped and nearly fell in the water, and would have done so had Eli not caught at his arm and dragged him forward on to the cabin-top. Everyone roared with laughter. It was a great joke, a great sign of happiness, that Mr. Blossom was tight and merry enough to dance along his top-plank at ten o'clock on a rainy night.

6

I t was the following evening. We were tied up at Fenny
Stratford, the six-inch lock which had been made necessary,
we were told, by a mistake in engineering. Whether this was
true or not we never knew, but according to the story the
engineer who had made this notable error of judgment afterwards, in despair, committed suicide by jumping in the canal.

All day it had rained. Now, with the hatches tight shut and
the stove roaring red, the heat in the cabin of the *Ariadne* was
almost painful. Emma, dressed only in cotton pyjama trousers,
was cooking the supper. Charity was writing to her step-
father. Nanette was lying on her back in the motor cabin
reading *Good-bye to Berlin*.

'. . . . we forgot to set the alarm,' wrote Charity, 'and over-
slept. So the Blossoms got away ahead of us, which was quite a
good thing I expect, because they do go faster. . . .'

Eli had waved his hand at Nanette's rumpled head peeping
sleepily over the cabin-top and called out:

'See you in Brumagum.'

And Nanette, waving back, had promised to be there.

The previous night she had given him her card with a
London telephone number and the name of a Mayfair club
printed in one corner. She had felt this was the right thing to

do, but had not told either Emma or Charity, anticipating contempt. The card lay in an inside pocket of Eli's jacket, from where it was brought out many times to be shown round as a trophy of a very high order, becoming, as the weeks passed, more and more dirty and dog-eared but never losing in dignity, and there, in the same inside pocket of Eli's jacket, it probably is to-day.

Our life at this time was a simple matter of desire and gratification; the needs were not exorbitant, and the fulfilment of them, therefore, came naturally and easily. Each day we tired our bodies out, and through each day looked forward to the pleasure of rest and sleep. Open air and exercise sharpened our hungers to a point of undiscriminating greed, and our evening supper, the only meal we could eat without anxiety or haste, was sufficient reward for all hardships endured. Our homes might be cramped, but they were ours. We were proud of them, as a schoolboy takes delight in his first study. And their comfort at night, with the engine stilled and the stove glowing, seemed truly, after an arduous day, a luxury defying comparison.

Our attention was daily absorbed by the trials of boating, the continual possibility of accidents, leaving us no margin for discontent. Of lovers or of marriage we thought but dimly, and felt as yet no craving for a companionship other than that we gave ourselves or found along the way. We were happy, and knew we were happy, being in a state ideal and rare when our living matched and even exceeded our youthful expectation of what life might be. We were utterly healthily selfish and, not realizing this, escaped the sophisticated poison of guilt.

'. . . . it rained,' wrote Charity, 'all day, and half-way through the morning the engine suddenly stopped. . . .'

It had suddenly stopped. Luckily we were near a depot, one of the two that existed between London and Birmingham to deal

66

with repairs and breakdowns. Emma had bicycled there for help, the engine being within our scope only as far as starting and stopping it were concerned.

The engineer who took charge of her was a tall man in horn-rimmed spectacles called Joe, with a long face and long humorous lines accentuating its length. She told him that the engine had stopped for no apparent reason and refused to start again. She told him where the boats were lying. He listened in silence, nodding. Presently her bicycle was pushed inside a small van and she was being driven back to the cut by a roundabout route.

It was an almost forgotten experience to bounce along a main road in a car and had all the charm of a stolen treat. Once, his eyes on the road ahead, Joe took his glasses off and handed them to Emma, asking her to wipe them clear. The gesture, absent-minded as it was, startled her oddly. She took the glasses, and as she obediently rubbed them clean she thought, still with a sense of shock: 'This is what wives do.' Some curtain stirred; some mist lifted a very little; some hint of a world private and particular touched her like the fringe of a spicy breeze. She rubbed the glasses, and rubbed the glasses, straining too hard to capture what was still only a ghost in her own mind. But through the day that insignificant gesture and the ripple of sensation it produced in her persistently recurred, arousing a faint and nostalgic pleasure, and a fainter but living curiosity.

We watched Joe while he unscrewed brass cocks and fiddled his hands dirty, Emma and Nanette squeezed into the engine-hole opposite him, Charity crouched on the gunwale outside with rain flicking against her oilskin and into her bent face, all of us silently awaiting the magic remedy. He diagnosed an airlock in the feed-pipe and very quickly put the matter right. Rubbing his hands on a grease rag, he looked up from face to face, shaking his head and smiling secretly.

'What's the joke?' we asked him.

'You ought to be able to straighten out an air-lock your-selves,' he said gently.

'No one ever showed us how.'

'Well, you'll know next time, won't you?' he said, still briskly rubbing his hands.

We nodded, doubting if we should. He started up the engine with a single flick of the wrist and, refusing to stay for a cup of tea, climbed into his van, backed in a semi-circle of leaping mud, and shot away over the bridge and out of sight.

It was always difficult to get going again after such a stoppage: limbs had stiffened and chilled in the interval, water had clammily crept inside our collars. We spurred ourselves forward with grim austerity, and the morning crept on, accelerated, had quite suddenly it seemed, gone by us. We crossed Tring Summit, that lovely winding stretch of water, where the wind was shut away from us by high steep banks hung with almost tropical creepers and lush undergrowth, and the rain fell with kinder intention, a glitter of Spring in its mistiness. Like an outrider escorting us courteously through a foreign country, a kingfisher glinted ahead, pausing to wait with brilliant stillness until we drew nearly level, then again springing out from the side in a wide blue arc and speeding on. The water was rich with confused green reflections, as if even beneath the surface vegetation profusely grew, and, although the motor allowed no noises beyond its own, from the butty we could hear blackbirds singing. A heron turned its long neck towards us and flapped up on lonely wings.

On the other side of the Summit the ground fell away, and the locks for the first time took us downhill. The boats, instead of rising up, sank down with the emptying water. There was a new danger to be avoided, for at the bottom of every lock was a sill, and boats as they fell were inclined to drift backwards, their sterns becoming stranded on the sill while their bows still sank. A boat, in such a way, could break her back, and we had for so long been going uphill that this particular peril was forgotten and it was only a terrified cry from Charity that saved us from disaster. The *Venus* had been left slightly in gear, and so automatically kept herself ahead, but the *Ariadne*, unattended, had floated back and was caught on the slimy sill. Her back quarters were already heaving themselves grotesquely into the air, her whole length sloping downwards in a dangerous nose-dive. We tore round the lock and across the gates, in maddened haste winding paddles up, dropping others, preventing further water from wasting away and pouring more in at the other end to float the *Ariadne* free. In our confusion we wound the wrong paddles, and dropped the ones we should have raised and screamed across at one another and all but died of worry. However, in the end the lock was again half-filled; the *Ariadne* righted herself and lifted clear of the sill, and we breathed once more.

Thoroughly flustered by this accident, Emma, after checking the butty at the next lock, tied her to a bollard as though in an uphill lock. It was an elementary mistake: the water declined and the rope, unable to bear the whole strain of boat and cargo, snapped in two. Emma was horrified.

'I must be mad,' she cried. 'How could I be so stupid?' Charity said nothing. Nanette was ahead, lock-wheeling.

We were passing close to an aerodrome. The country here was flat and spacious, spreading away to far hills, and patterned like light and shade with generous many-coloured fields. Flocks of Americans crossed the bridges wearing fur-lined flying-suits, or with their crazy caps turned the wrong way round on their heads. Many were riding bicycles. They watched us, some of them, with the cold-hearted interest of the foreigner. One or two called out: 'Hi there,' and one threw down a packet of cigarettes.

Nanette came bicycling back, flung her machine aboard and herself after it.

'Boats coming,' she said. 'Four locks ready for us, glory be. Have a Lucky Strike,' she added, pulling out a packet.

'Oh' said Charity, 'did you meet some Americans too?'

'Yes,' said Nanette, with downcast eyes, 'aren't they kind?'

Aeroplanes were droning out of sight in the grey sky. Nanette stood beside Emma on the gunwale of the *Venus*, and leaning her chin in her hands talked of her mother, who was dead. Emma was distressed by her off-hand manner.

'Didn't you like your mother?' she asked.

Nanette was silent. Then she said: 'I was never quite sure if she liked me. I wanted her to notice me more. Children do want to be noticed, especially little girls. She was beautiful. I think she was probably very beautiful. People used to say to me "your lovely mother". But when you're little that isn't what matters, in fact it's rather frightening. It gets in the way, if you know what I mean.' There was a pause. 'She was never at home,' said Nanette. 'She was always away, or abroad. I was fourteen when she died. I was at school and she was in France. I'd like to see her now,' she said, frowning. 'I'd feel differently now. It's such a nuisance, it's too late.'

An otter swam across in front of our bows. We watched the two straight ripples flooding back from its moving head; then it dived.

'What will you do when you leave the cut?' asked Emma.

'What are you going to do when the war's over?'

'I don't know. I think I'd like to go to Egypt.'

'Egypt?'

'Nice and hot there. Or India. Only India's so far from London. I think I'd rather go to Egypt. What will you do?'

'I don't know,' said Emma.

In her head danced a dream-vision of the Sahara desert, mixed up with the South of France and smart dying women and London night-clubs. She sat up on the edge of the cabin-top with legs dangling, steering the *Venus* with one blue hand. Nanette's words conjured up for her that possible time, the future. Like a hobby for spare thought, the image of it, blurred and unreal, was always lurking at the back of her mind; within its bubble frame lived a quantity of headless creatures who, with decided voices and actions, promised her any amount of glamour and instruction.

We skirted a grassy corner where weeping willows bent treacherously down to embrace us, and there, huddled on the wet bank, was a man fishing.

'Caught anything?' called out Nanette.

'Not yet,' he answered.

The lock came bleakly into sight, a grey stone cottage standing back to one side of it, miles from any other house. Emma slid to her feet and stood leaning forward, focusing her attention on the business ahead.

'You know,' she said, wiping back the wet hair from her eyes. 'I can't really imagine doing anything else but this. Not *really*, I mean. We make plans, but they aren't real plans. I feel we shall always go on, sweating up and down the cut, in the rain, like to-day.'

'Well, we won't,' said Nanette, 'but it's nice enough while it lasts.'

That afternoon Cleopatra fell into the cut and almost drowned. We were battling with the Jackdaw Pound, a length of water made up of aggravating bends curving snakily back, one upon the other. We were going cautiously, blowing the horns at every corner, thrusting the tillers hard across from side to side. Charity suddenly thought the cat should have some air. She brought out the unwilling animal and set it on the cabin-top of the butty, where it cowered away from the rain and cast malignant glances all about it. Just then we were nearing a bridge-hole, and Emma on the motor turned round and held up two fingers, at the same time signing Nanette to run on the mud. Charity, occupied in mother-craft, was at that moment leaning anxiously across the reach of Nanette's tiller, saying: 'Oh Cleopatra, do be careful . . .' and Nanette was crying: 'Charity, how can I steer – for goodness sake get out of the way.'

71

All at the same time, it seemed, the butty had slammed forward into the stern of the *Venus*, whose bows, swinging sideways with the impact, were soundly knocked by the motor-boat just then emerging from under the bridge, and Cleopatra, quite taken by surprise, was jolted overboard. Charity, too late, made a wild grab following it with a cry so terrible that it might indeed have been her own child that was drowning. The *Ariadne* continued to shove herself rudely forward. The boaters were yelling.

'You silly cat,' shouted Nanette. Charity, her eyes stretched wide with anguish, was tearing off her oilskin and snatching at the laces of her boots.

'Don't be an ass,' cried Nanette, shaking her by the arm. 'You can't go in, it's too cold, it's madness – look, look – there's no need, she's swimming – look at the little beast, much better than I can. Hurray, come on, this way, this way.'

'. . . . Cleopatra,' wrote Charity to her step-father that evening, 'swam like anything. Most cats don't, you know, but Cleopatra is different from them – she is a fine swimmer, and also very brave. . . .'

Nanette, to encourage the kitten, pushed out the short shaft towards her, but Cleopatra misunderstood the intention and frightened by the splash it made, turned away and struck out with increased desperation towards the middle of the cut.

'You fool,' screamed Nanette.

Charity, with tears rolling down her nose, was again beginning to undress. But this drama was being attended closely by the boaters who had bumped us. The steerer of the motor, like a decent saviour, guided in his boat to head the feeble creature off, and then his son, a dirty-faced child of ten or twelve, knelt down on their cargo of coal and leaning far out scooped the dripping, clawing, snarling kitten up and waved her in the air. More, he jumped off at the next bridge-hole, which was a good quarter mile further on, and came running back along the tow-path to return her. Nanette gave him a packet of tea in gratitude, and this he grabbed without a word, grinning, and scampered away again. Cleopatra turned her flamy eyes once towards Charity and then fell to licking herself in front of the stove.

'You were crying,' said Nanette in surprise.

'It was nerves,' answered Charity, quite calm again. 'That, and imagination. I thought of her dead and it seemed so horrid.'

'But we see enough dead dogs floating down the cut, and they really do look beastly, and you don't cry over them.'

'That's different. I never knew them. And anyway they look *so* beastly, blown out like balloons with their legs in the air, I never think of them as dogs, just as something nasty.'

'It isn't logical,' said Nanette. 'You must be terribly senti-mental.'

'Perhaps I am,' said Charity indifferently. 'I often cry.'

'I never do,' said Nanette.

By this time the boats were moving again. Charity, instead of putting on her oilskin, stayed below and cut thick slices of bread and spread them thickly with jam, and made the tea. She also heated a saucerful of milk for Cleopatra. There were three more locks and then another stretch of water, and then we had reached Fenny Stratford where we decided to lie for the night.

Immediately beside the lock was a pub, and in this pub we could buy provisions, including tins of milk and vegetables and bread. Leaving Charity and Nanette to make fast the boats, Emma went inside to do the shopping. It was just beginning to grow dark. The flames from a huge coal fire flung reddish reflections on the back of the wooden settle and along the glossy counter. She stamped her wet boots con-tentedly in front of it and watched the pools of water form around her on the floor.

'Beans,' she said, 'are always very useful. I'd like two tins of beans, and a tin of salmon, and we need about twelve tins of milk. And rations for three. And a loaf.'

The cheerful fat woman who owned the pub clattered down the tins in a row and went away to fetch the bread. She switched the wireless on as she left the room; somewhere in England a dance-band was playing: 'I'll See You in My Dreams.' Holding out her hands to the fire, Emma crouched down humming the tune. Her hands were ingrained with dirt, the nails broken, callouses were forming on the palms. Her mind relaxed in steamy warmth, empty, uncaring.

A man came into the pub, unmistakably a boater.

'Those your boats outside?' he asked.

Emma said they were. He told her that he and his mate were lying the other side of the lock on their way down to London. He was a middle-aged man with a shrewd face and a rasping voice. His name was Freddie. Presently his mate arrived, a boy much younger with lustrous eyes, who nodded at Emma without speaking. She went to the door and looked out at the dim hooded greyish shapes of the boats.

'Hi,' she called. Charity leaned out from the engine-hole.

'Come and have a drink. There's a lovely fire in here. It's warm.'

Charity shook her head, holding up her two arms which were coated as high as the elbows with thick satiny black oil.

'I dropped the priming-tool in the bilges. So stupid of me.'

Accidents never made her angry; she bore them patiently.

'Perhaps I'll come along when I'm clean,' she called, and disappeared again.

Nanette was filling both the water-cans at the wayside tap. They were so heavy she had to make two journeys, her short roundabout figure struggling forward through rain and mud and increasing darkness, the water-can clumsily bumping against her leg and spilling at every step.

Freddie came up to Emma and touched her shoulder. 'Matthew was wondering if you'd write a letter to his young lady for him.'

'Of course I will,' said Emma.

Matthew looked at the floor, blinking his long lashes. She carried the tins of food and milk over to the *Ariadne* and came back with a pen and a block of paper. Matthew and she sat side by side on the settle. Emma waited. At last she said:

'What do you want me to write?'

'Dear Rose,' said he in a low voice.

'Dear Rose,' – she wrote, and waited. He was silent.

'What shall I say next?'

'Will be in Brum next Saturday. Hope to see you then.' She wrote this down.

'Is that all? Isn't there anything else you want to say?' She stared at him urgently, trying to force upon him the fire of a lover. He was dumb and unhappy.

'Love from Matthew?' she asked. He nodded.

Nanette burst in, flapping and shuddering. 'Ugh, what a beastly cold wet night. My stomach feels cold. I'm going to have a rum. Emma, have a rum?'

We were the only four people in the pub. The fire leapt up with intimate joy, like the blaze at a children's party. Nanette came across with a glass in her hand, her oilskin swinging open to show the bulging mass of scarves and jersies inside.

'What are you doing?' she cried.

'You must put a row of kisses at the bottom,' said Emma, handing the pen to Matthew. 'Go on. Think how they'll please her.'

Quite suddenly his dark young strangely-suffering face broke into a smile of excitement. He clenched his fingers round the pen and added at the foot of the page a row of heavy crosses. Nanette leaned over Emma's shoulder to watch. Freddie came strolling up with a pint of beer.

'Rose can't read neither,' he said, 'but her Mum can. Her Mum's a scholar.'

Matthew was laughing and wagging his head. We had a beer all round and told them of Cleopatra's adventure. In return they repeated stories of the cats they had known, and dogs of theirs that had drowned, and the times they themselves had fallen in, and the body they once picked up in their blades.

'Guts,' said Freddie, narrowing his eyes. 'You should 'a seen 'em. Yards on 'em, wound around the prop they was like a string of sausages. Man or woman, no one could tell in the finish, but 'e was drownded any road. Held us up two days that did, we had to 'tend the inquest and Matthew was took sick. It was the guts turned 'im.' Matthew looked green at the memory. ''E had to have a physic.'

They told us that a drowned woman floated face downwards, and a man on his back. Emma tore herself away from their feast of reminiscence and went back to the butty to cook supper. Here she found Charity lying full length on her unrolled bedding; she was writing a letter and looked up mildly as Emma scrambled down.

'There's a kettle of hot water,' she said, 'I thought perhaps you'd like to wash before supper, and then I can wash afterwards.' As Emma said nothing, she added: 'I think we *ought* to wash to-night. We didn't yesterday, and not much the day before.'

'Oh, all right,' said Emma. She emptied the kettle into a small bowl and washed herself very quickly all over. The water showered out to left and right, sizzling on the stove, splashing the side-bed. Her skin at the end felt sticky and stiff from the drying soap. She poured away the brownish scum left at the bottom of the bowl, hung the bowl up on a hook, and opened a tin of beans. Nanette jumped aboard and bent her head in through the hatches.

'Look,' she said. 'I've bought a new length of cotton-line off Freddie. I know we don't really want it, but he was so

76

insistent, and after all those stories it was difficult to refuse.' She threw it on the cabin-top. 'When's supper?'

'In ten minutes. I'll shout when it's ready.'

Charity looked up from her corner. 'How do you spell "conscientious"?' she asked.

'I never know,' said Emma, stirring away at the frying-pan. 'Lord, ain't it hot?'

'Emma' wrote Charity in the chronicle to her step-father, 'is wearing pink pyjamas, and her face is even redder, so she looks red all over.' After a moment of thought she added: 'We are just going to have supper – beans and bacon. With lots of love from Charity.'

After supper Nanette read out extracts from *Good-bye to Berlin*. Charity, not attending, sat cross-legged trying to play *Greensleeves* on a comb.

'How are your bugs?' asked Emma, interrupting.

'Awful,' said Nanette, looking up from the book. 'I've hardly complained at all but I'm covered in bites. Luckily they don't seem to bite my face much.'

'It's funny they don't come into this cabin.'

'I expect they will,' said Nanette. 'I wish they would; it doesn't seem fair to stick to me.'

'Well, we've got mice instead. I heard them last night.'

'What, with Cleopatra about? She's a lot of use.'

'Cleopatra isn't a killer,' said Charity, taking her lips away from the comb. 'She's an affectionate cat.'

'If you like,' said Emma to Nanette, 'you can stay in bed a bit longer to-morrow morning. There aren't any locks for over an hour, so there's no need for three of us to get up.'

'It's hardly a pleasure to stay in bed now,' said Nanette peevishly, 'with these bugs. They wake me up at night, and even when I'm asleep I can feel them running over me.'

Emma lay flat on her back with her legs stretched vertically

77

up the wooden wall in front of her, arms folded beneath her head. Reaching out one hand she could touch the shelf of tattered books; reaching out the other she could poke the fire. Swollen with sleep, she did neither. 'Charity,' she said, 'play something different.'

Charity went on playing *Greensleeves*.

'I wish you'd stop,' said Nanette crossly. 'It's not musical. How can I read?'

Charity looked at her blankly over the edge of her comb.

'You are obstinate,' said Nanette.

Late that night Charity awoke from a deep sleep and lay in her damp corner wondering why. A great stillness surrounded her. The butty scraped lightly against the canal side with the exhausted peace of a convalescent. Then she realized: the rain had stopped and Cleopatra, who usually slept across her neck, was gone. She wriggled into a dressing-gown and climbed out into the rainy hatches. The sky was full of stars. There was no wind. Facing her across the cabin-top was a large rat.

'Oh,' she said loudly, and the rat bobbed out of sight. 'Cleopatra,' she called in a whisper.

Then she noticed that the new cotton-line bought by Nanette that evening for eight-and-six, no longer lay on the butty. The cabin-top was bare, shining in the starlight. She looked up at the sky; it was empty of clouds and faintly ominous. Freddie had passed by the boats at ten o'clock on his way back from the pub, and called out 'Good-night.' No one else had been along the tow-path.

In her bare feet she padded along, past the black solid shapes of the lock, to where Freddie's boats were lying. On the roof of his butty lay a cotton-line; she was sure it was the same one. It looked in the starlight brand-new, still tied together. But as she leaned fearfully forward, peering, a watch-dog sprawling beside it raised one ear at her and growled. She hurried on.

'He must think we're fools,' she thought. 'What an easy trick.'

She paused by the fore-deck, shivering with cold and fear. There, in front of her nose, close to her hand, was a long thick rope, neatly coiled together. With a vague nightmare guiltiness she bent and picked it up and hung it on her shoulder, expecting the dog at every second to explode into savage barking. The mud oozed up between her toes. She tiptoed back, wiped her feet on the grass, and taking the rope down with her into the cabin, climbed back to bed and immediately fell asleep.

7

B y next morning the sky had clouded thickly over. No rain fell but it was very cold in a peculiar still way. Cleopatra was asleep across Charity's feet when she woke up. Freddie's boats had gone. She told us of the night's piracy and we looked at her in admiration.

'You are brave Charity,' said Emma. 'I could *never* have done it. Supposing the dog had chased you, or Freddie had heard?'

'The dog was chained, and I was very quiet. Anyway, supposing he *had* heard – I was only taking his rope because he stole our line. He stole first of all.'

It was true: Charity did have a calmly heroic streak in her, allied perhaps to her sense of justice, which was strong.

Nanette roared with laughter. 'What a nerve he had,' she said, 'I do admire him. He thought we were suckers, and suckers deserve to be fooled. But I'm glad we had the last joke.'

It was Sunday. Politely along the tow-path stepped the couples in their fancy clothes. Men and boys of every age patiently crouched on the banks, fishing, their bicycles and wicker baskets cast down in the grass beside them. They looked at us sullenly, for our passing disturbed the fish they never caught. Nanette steered the butty-boat, with *Good-bye to Berlin* spread open on the slide of the hatches in front of her, weighed down with a windlass; the butty wavered from side to side across the cut under her haphazard guidance. Emma sat on the cabin-top splicing the rope she had broken the previous day. Charity, with Cleopatra for company, was steering the motor. Now and again, as we passed near villages, we heard the church bells ringing.

A boy on the tow-path, with a knapsack and bare legs, called out to Charity: 'Will you give me a lift, miss?'

She told him to walk on to the next bridge-hole, and here she picked him up.

'Aren't you cold?' she asked, looking at his strong hairy legs.

'Yes,' he said. 'I am; but it makes a nice change.' He was a mechanic, he told her, on leave from the Air Force, stationed in the Middle East.

'Rain,' he said, 'is something I've dreamed about. These last few days have been like heaven.' He was spending his leave in walking.

'Where?' she asked.

'Anywhere,' he said. 'It all looks good to me.' He came from Leeds. 'I love England,' he said in his flat unemphatic accent. 'You don't know what it's like till you get sent away from it. All these trees and cows and stuff.'

She looked at him seriously, feeling ignorant and slightly ashamed. To be far away and homesick in a hot country was something she felt she should have experienced. She guessed they were much the same age, but he had been more severely handled and had developed beyond her.

'I wouldn't mind having your job,' he said.

'It's very hard work.'

'You're kidding,' he said, and taking the tiller-handle from her steered the *Venus* on the next half-mile. Before stepping off he offered her, in fairness, a shilling, which she equally gravely refused. Nanette, when she later told her of this, was amazed and reproachful.

'You didn't take it? The price of two half-pints. . . . ?'

82

'He may be dead in a month,' said Charity, throwing her long dark hair back with a wild open gesture. 'How could I take a shilling from him?'

She had longed, when he left her, to give him a charm, to be able to protect him.

'So long,' he had called, hoisting on his knapsack.

'So long,' she answered. She would do something, she thought with her heart bounding, she would write to him; but he left her no address, no name, no sign of himself.

Later, as the boats were passing a farm, she made one of her astonishing leaps and just reached the bank.

'I don't know how you do it,' shouted Nanette. 'One day of course you won't, and serve you right.' Charity waved back at her cheerfully and disappeared through a gap in the hedge.

Nanette, immersed in her book, failed to see Emma's signal and, taking the butty carelessly round a bend, came into almost headlong collision with another boat. The butty heeled far over to one side, the water rocking round it. A dull whining groan came from the steel in the hold.

There was a woman aboard the motor-boat polishing brass. 'Yer soppy date,' she screamed at Nanette as the two of them came abreast. Her husband, steering, was silent. Nanette disliked her wizened evil little face.

'You're a silly old prune yourself,' she shouted back.

It was like putting a match to a rocket. A stream of invective burst from her mouth, her voice, as the boats drew apart, growing more and more shrill. She snatched a mop from the cabin-top and passionately shook it. Nanette, delightedly defiant, waved her fists and her book in reply.

Charity reappeared, holding in her cap six eggs, and carefully stepped aboard at the next bridge-hole.

'Look,' she said, 'two eggs each for supper.'

Nanette described her passage of arms.

'She'll hate you for life,' said Charity doubtfully. 'Hate you and hate you. It's awfully dangerous.'

'Oh, bother her,' said Nanette impatiently. 'I don't care. She was rude to me.'

'Well, you did bump her boat.'

'Yes, I know I did, and I bumped it because I was reading, and I shouldn't be reading when I'm steering. Don't be a prig, Charity.' After that she was sulky for some time.

We met towards the end of the morning some of our brethren, three girls whose weary anxious faces spoke of trouble past and greater trouble expected. With a certain constraint we saluted one another. Their appearance discouraged us. We watched them creep doggedly away out of sight behind.

'They do look in a bad way,' said Nanette, 'I don't want to suffer like that.'

The same afternoon Emma ran the motor aground on mud. It was the first really bad encounter with mud we had had. Mud, with which in the future we were so often to come to grips, assumed for the first time the sinister importance of an enemy, to be feared and hated as though it were a sensible thing. We struggled and heaved, leaning our whole weight on the shafts until those stout poles bent and splinters ran into our fingers. Protesting groans were forced out of our mouths as we strained every muscle beyond its capacity. After twenty minutes of fruitless agony, we had decided that nothing on earth would ever move us again. We were in a deserted part of the country, far from friendly humans; moorhens scuttered about on the water, cheeping. In the hedges the buds were fattening towards April. The sky above was thick and still. The afternoon was very cold. We rested despairingly in this muddy lowering solitude, and Nanette cried:

'Listen. . . .'

Faint but distinct on the silent air came the patter of an engine.

'Boats,' said Charity. 'They're behind us. They're catching us up.'

Again we flung ourselves upon the shafts, and the *Venus* unaccountably shifted an inch or so. Emma reversed the engine; again we pushed. The *Venus* backed clear away off the mud. Nanette and Charity leapt aboard the drifting butty and at the same moment round the bend came the pair of boats we had heard.

'Go *on*,' shouted Nanette. 'Don't let them pass. Go on, we're free.'

Emma hesitated, wondering what she ought to do. The boats were close and quickly coming closer. In the end she waved them past her, and stuck out her lip at Nanette's angry and disappointed face. The boats were crewed by three elderly women and one very old man. They looked at Emma as they passed, amusement screwed silently up in their weathered eyes. They had the appearance of four tough battered little gnomes, and the name they shared through blood or marriage was Silver.

'We were stuck on the mud,' shouted Emma, to explain the weakness they were certain to be despising.

They chorused back the boater's stock answer: 'Oh-ah,' hardly troubling in their haste and contempt to slow their boats down to a civil speed.

As we started up in their wake, something damp and soft fell against Emma's cheek. It was not rain, but a snow-flake. Others followed it down. The reason for the coldly brooding sky was explained in a dense flurry of white, and after only a few moments the beetle-like tarpaulin body of the *Venus* was overcome and wrapped in snow, and the vivid scarlet of the water-can nearly suppressed underneath a clinging coat of whiteness. Emma looked round at the other two through what appeared to be a dazzling swarm of insects, seeming, in the air, paradoxically black. They danced and spun and whirled in a mad profusion, yet each flake, individually followed with the eye, came slipping slowly down on a pausing dubious path to touch, not sharply, but with melting tenderness on whatever it chanced to fall. Nanette and Charity waved at her through the flutter, laughing with astonishment, and Emma waved in reply, swinging her arms round and round to keep off the soft attackers.

Soon the tunnel of Stoke shut off from us not only the snow, but air and light and landscape, almost life itself. Like blinded wretches we crept into its mouth of doom, a round opening low down in the side of a round high hill that might have been Proserpina's last sight of loving earth.

The headlights were switched on. Looking back, Emma could see the orange eye of the butty following, and its bulky shape silhouetted against the dwindling half-moon of the entrance. Then the boats turned a slight bend and all shapes were lost. Only ahead glittered a faint path on the black water, and above the bows of the motor could dimly be seen the wall arching over in a slimy prison. Monster drips, ice-cold, fell sometimes singly, sometimes in a sour rain. The bricks skinned her knuckles if she pushed the tiller too far out to right or left. The tunnel was crowded with the loud beat of the engine, banging away in the stagnant darkness with unnatural bravado.

Then the motor-boat passed under an air-vent and light fell in a shaft of scored and sunless severity from the earth above. Emma blinked her eyes in a flood of brilliance. Medieval angels might have been singing in its rigid glory, so fabulous, so inhuman did it seem. She watched the butty, foot by foot pass through its bluish beam, and saw for a moment Charity's stark white face irradiated, like a soul damned in wickedness tormented by a vision of heavenly joy. And again darkness; and the shattering noise of the engine; the sound of unseen water splashing underneath, and the repeated blundering crash of boat against wall. Light became synonymous with life; space was beauty. Then the butty head-lamp failed. Emma cut down her engine and shouted:

'Charity – your light: it's out.'

86

'What?' shouted Charity. 'I can't hear.' Her voice in the pitch dark was as grotesque as the huge shadow of a hand flung on a wall by candlelight.

'YOUR LIGHT'S GONE OUT.'

Charity said hurriedly: 'Nanette, give me the hurricane lamp. Our head-light's out.'

'How ghastly,' said Nanette. 'Are you going to take it up?' The boats were idling along and the water, softly lapping, seemed, with the noise and speed reduced, more menacing, peopled with crocodiles.

'Yes,' said Charity. 'Oh look – oh quick – how awful.'

Nanette screwed herself out of the cabin and took the tiller. Somewhere ahead, at what distance it was impossible to judge, a light the colour and size of a match flickered to meet us. Boats were approaching. Seizing the lantern, Charity hoisted herself to the roof of the cabin and began to crawl on hands and knees along the top-planks. The butty bumped against the side and she had to clutch a string to save herself.

'Oh Charity,' cried Nanette. 'I'm sorry. Are you still there?'

The orange spark was growing bigger; ahead of it in the water spilled out a fiery lengthening path. Emma blew her horn and its long echoing note was musically answered like a continuing echo. In that dead air the dying sound of horns was rich and sad, and the darkness was choked with smoke and the huge drumming of the two engines. Charity crawled hastily on, and reaching the foredeck crouched down with the lantern between her knees. Every few minutes a spatter of drops fell coldly on her head and hands and neck. Emma was hugging the motor along the right-hand wall; Nanette was doing the same with the butty. The two motor-boats came abreast of one another and edged slowly past with hardly a foot to spare. Emma called out the boater's greeting: 'How d'you do,' and had a gruff reply from the dim anonymous shape that passed so closely by her. The butty slid wraith-like after it; more greetings and a joke and a cackle from the crow-voiced woman, and then the dark meeting was over and the boats were drawing apart.

Each of us longed in a queer strained way to be free of this suffocating womb of rotting bricks; each of us nursed a primitive fear. To each of us occurred a flame of anguish, sprung out of fear, for the numberless creatures hidden away for years from the sun, victims of ancient cruelty, prisoners of our own day outrageously denied our day, men buried or breathing, past present or future, who cried out for their wasting eyes to be blinded by sunrise or blessed by sunset. Sympathy is a cowardly thing, and most easily forgotten.

After forty minutes of prayer, we were free. No bigger than the head of a pin we saw the farther opening. And it grew and grew, reflection making a full round circle of it, a sixpence, a shilling, a shining crown. We slid out into a sweet daylight, amazed to find it snowing. For we had forgotten the weather, and, in our pitchy black, thought of day as golden and leafy, with birds singing. As it was, the air and earth were blonde with falling and fallen snow and seemed even more dazzling, and fairer.

Only a little farther on, when the charm of freedom was already beginning to pall, Emma sighted a pair of boats tied snugly up outside a pub. It was the Silvers, who had decided that the day was too foul for further travelling. Their hatches were shut. The butty tiller was reversed and gently swinging. Greyish smoke blew up from the twin chimney-pots to battle with the pearly dropping snow. It was a scene of comfort Emma prepared herself to copy. But a shout from the tow-path made her turn her head. There was Nanette panting along and urgently waving one hand. Emma slowed down.

'What's the matter?'

'Let's pass them. Let's go on.'

'Oh Nanette, it's Sunday and snowing.'

'Yes I know, but we ought not to have let them by us. We ought to be more resolute,' screamed Nanette, cupping her hands round her mouth. 'Let's show them. Let's go on.'

'It's nearly two hours to the next stopping-place. What does Charity say?'

'She says the same as me. I'm getting on at the next bridge-hole and you can go back and have some tea.'

Mr. Silver poked his head out as we passed and looked at us in silent disgust. In less than an hour it was beginning to grow dark, an early darkness hurried on by the storm. We could hardly make out the bridge-holes as we drew near them. Nanette each time switched on her headlamp for a few seconds to find her direction, and then turned it off again. The snow looked alarming in that momentary bright glare, and denser. Charity, her headlamp having failed, steered as well as she could and hoped for the best.

'Would you like me to put the hurricane lamp on the bows?' asked Emma.

'Wouldn't help. You need a searchlight to penetrate this.'

We forgot that our noble attempt was really only an effort to worst the poor old Silvers, and felt ourselves related in valour to Scott or Magellan or any famous adventurer. With total darkness the snow stopped falling. With total darkness we met the first pair of fly-boats and realized our stupidity.

'My God,' said Emma. 'They'll run us down.'

The fly-boats, travelling all night by custom, had shaded headlamps. Our own lights were unprotected and the black-out regulations at that time were severely observed. In great haste Emma lit the hurricane lamp and slithered up to the bows, where she squatted down and wrapped it half about with her coat. Nanette blew her horn and winked her head-light on and off in warning.

The beer-boats passed us by without a crash.

'There's another pair behind us,' yelled the steerer of the butty.

We met the second pair in the darkest possible place, passing through a town where tall warehouses blocked out the sky which was just beginning to lighten with a moony radiance. We were afraid of the bridge-holes and the bends when they could then run us down before they had a chance to see us or we them. This was very nearly what happened. Nanette had cleared a bridge and was out the other side, when we heard her yell:

'Look out – the beer.'

Almost at once a narrow snout was thrusting round into the side of the butty while she still wallowed under the archway. Nanette, too late, was blowing her horn; there was a screaming of gears suddenly reversed and a voice shouting: 'Yer silly boogers.'

We thought it better to answer nothing: darkness which had delivered us into danger, now protected us. We heard Nanette hysterically laughing.

'I hope those are the last,' said Emma. 'Next time we'll sink.'

But Charity, thinking of her Air Force mechanic, had the impression of somehow discharging a debt to him by our folly. She felt a little mad with satisfaction, and almost longed to sink.

In fact, we met no more fly-boats but by this time we were cold with fear, cold with strain. Our eyes were stretched widely open as though by mere size they could pierce the darkness and warn us of danger. We had to cross an aqueduct and this was trial by water indeed, for the parapet on either side was no more than a foot or so high and the river which we spanned was far below. We had the feeling that the butty, if she crashed the side would ride straight across that flimsy parapet and fall, fall – it was too horrible to contemplate. Nanette, who from the motor could see the butty bows more clearly than we on the butty could, called back directions:

'To the left, to the LEFT – you're in the middle now, keep straight, keep on. . . .'

We crossed that narrow air-borne channel with cold hands and sick hearts and were glad when we reached the other side, with whitish trees growing in firm earth, and good mud banks to border us.

We were tired, too tired to talk. Around us glimmered the snow, more and more clearly, and the branches of trees, instead of overshadowing, seemed to cast light upon us. Cleopatra came out and stalked delicately about on top of the cabin, leaving crisp little markings where her feet had been. Then, only a couple of hundred yards or so from the foot of Buckby locks where we were going to tie, Nanette ran the motor across a submerged tree-trunk and we were stuck again.

It was very silent. The only sounds we heard were our own groans as we pushed at the shafts, and the throbbing of the engine. Once or twice we nearly gave it up and went to bed, leaving the boats just as they were in the middle of the cut. But instead we persisted, our boots slipping in the wet snow, the night beautiful, the sky alive with stars above us. It took us half an hour to divorce ourselves from that miserable stump of wood. We limped on and tied the boats below the bottom lock of the flight. The ropes when we knotted them were half-frozen, stiff in our raw hands. Charity, standing on the gunwale outside, stretched one long leg into the engine hole and stopped the motor with the toe of her boot. At once the night was black and white and soundless, perfectly still.

A stew had all the day been cooking itself with delicious fragrance on top of the stove, but we were hardly strong enough to enjoy it. Our eyes were watering with fatigue, our mouths already dry with the need of sleep. We nearly went to bed in our boots and certainly no attempt was made at washing.

Nanette said: 'Well, we've got a good two-hour start on the Silvers.'

Until she mentioned them, we had forgotten the Silvers.

91

8

A harassing day lay ahead of us. We began it in cheerful ignorance. The sky was blue, the morning snow was sunny and gay. We started on the flight of seven locks as light-hearted as larks, and as the boats rose up from lock to lock, so our spirits lifted with them. The world was beautiful and we loved ourselves.

Then between the third and fourth lock we picked up something in our blades. The engine shuddered and coughed and then stopped. We shafted the *Venus* forward into the lock, filled the lock with water and then lay on our stomachs along the side, poking with shafts underneath the boat and despairing. A tall gaunt old lock-keeper came hobbling down the tow-path to help us.

'What's the matter then?' he said. We shook our heads. He took a shaft from us and with wrinkled expert hands twisted it out of sight under the water.

'Rope,' he said, 'That's what 'tis. You got a great old bit of rope around the prop.'

And to prove his words a few hairy strands of rope hung from the hook of the shaft when he drew it up. We hated having to worry, the day was so fair. One felt that under the snow were many flowers on the verge of appearing, their petals already open, yellow flowers of Spring like celandines. Where no one had trodden were the tracks of small animals, and the light hopping crosses of birds' feet, as though they were busy in the preparation of nests and summery songs. Nanette thought how nice it would be to lie on her back and finish reading *Good-bye to Berlin*. We lay, however, more uncomfortably on our stomachs and took it in turns to poke beneath the *Venus*. A lump of rope rewarded us now and again and such trophies we laid on the lock-side for encouragement. We could feel with the spike of the shaft a dull thick mass wound round the propeller, and this, in spite of the rope we hauled away from it, never seemed to get smaller.

'It wants cutting away with a knife,' said the old lock-keeper. 'That's what it wants. We ain't never going to get that away with a shaft.'

He began to talk of 'dropping 'er on the sill,' a long task and a dangerous one which would necessitate first of all turning the *Venus* round.

'We can't do that,' said Charity. 'We'll have to go in. After all, it isn't really *winter* now. Just because there's snow. . . .'

Her voice faded away. The sunlight was suddenly meretricious and the water dripping down from the shaft on our hands, achingly cold.

'I'll toss you for it,' said Emma.

'You needn't,' said Charity. 'I'll go in anyway, if you like. Some people bathe all the year round.'

But Emma, feeling she was due for the sweets of heroism, tossed a halfpenny. Charity said 'heads' and the coin fell tails. Emma put on a pair of dungarees and a cotton shirt.

'You mustn't stay in for more than a minute,' said Charity. 'I'll time you.'

Holding by one hand to a loop of rope and with the bread knife in her other, Emma as quickly as possible submerged herself up to the chin in the bitter water. For a moment her mouth was filled by her fluttering heart; then she laid her cheek against the flank of the *Venus*, and reaching far underneath felt for the rope and began with hasty uneven strokes to saw away at it.

During the first fifteen seconds the cold gripping her all over was so intense she thought: 'I must die; I am dying.' Then she went numb, and no longer felt cold, and her mind was purged of everything except the necessity of blindly cutting through this rope. The other three watched her; Nanette very soberly, Charity with a fierce expression on her thin face as though her own spirit was under water, icily grappling, and the old man muttering aloud and spitting across his shoulder. Happening to raise her head, Nanette saw below a plume of smoke approaching. She pursed up her lips and was silent.

Emma lifted her livid face dripping out of the water and said: 'I think . . . I think . . .'

Her teeth were chattering, her lips blue above them. They dragged her aboard and pushed her into the cabin to dress. Nanette said in Charity's ear:

'Look – I believe it's the Silvers.'

Charity turned her startled eyes in the same direction. Together they watched the two long black boats just coming into sight.

'They must have started terribly early,' said Charity.

The old lock-keeper, who had gone on probing away by himself, gave a sudden hoarse whistling sound, twisted the shaft rapidly round and round and hauled out from the water a tattered piece of rope about four feet long.

'There you are,' he said. 'There you are; that's it – we got it. There you are.'

Charity looked into the butty cabin. 'Emma,' she said, 'are you ready to go? The Silvers are just behind us.'

We were three locks ahead of them. By the time we had started the engine and got ourselves going the distance had lessened to two locks. That is to say, we had about twenty minutes' advantage. With the old lock-keeper helping us, we rushed the boats up the remaining three locks, gates slamming behind us, water spouting ahead. Old Billy Silver came trundling up on his bicycle.

'You'll have to loose us by at the top,' he said.

'Why?' said Nanette.

'You're holding us up,' he said, blinking his reddish little eyes.

'Rubbish,' she answered. 'You catch us up first, then we'll see about loosing you by.'

He said no more for the moment but stood, five feet high, by his bicycle, with his bowed legs and his bowed back and venom in his ugly little face.

They chased us up the Buckby locks; they chased us through Braunston tunnel, they chased us down the other side. And all that day we fled before them like guilty creatures, casting glances over our shoulders and wishing the boats were horses that we might flog them faster.

We had, somehow, in spite of the menace behind us, to attend to other things. Charity, at the top of the Buckby locks, went leaping away with a jug and was back a minute later with fresh milk spilling over her hand and down her trousers. And at Norton Toll Office, where our trip-card was marked and the boats gauged, we found a batch of letters waiting for us.

Letters had a different significance in those days: we earned them. A regular post delivered at the door by a postman is a dull affair. But for people living in lonely places, islands or distant stations, the mail arriving at long intervals, once a week or perhaps only once a month, is very far from being dull. Letters then take on a new meaning, become not letters, but news. Any scrap of writing is the extension of a hand from a world out of touch, the translation of a voice from a world otherwise silent; no matter whose hand, or whose voice, it comes as a proof of living. So we, every now and then, broke from the jungly bounds of our canal to snatch up these precious waiting packages and feed on them like glamorous bread for the next few days. Charity had a telegram from her step-father.

'Is anything wrong?' asked Emma.

'No. He often sends me telegrams,' said Charity, her face alight. 'Long telegrams. He sends his love to both of you.'

'He doesn't know us,' said Nanette.

'He sends you his love all the same. And he says we're not to drink the water we've boiled our eggs in, like we've been doing – it'll give us warts. And he says at the end: "Do not despair." I wonder why he says that? I'm not despairing.'

'He sounds a bit off his head to me,' said Nanette.

Emma lock-wheeled on foot the six Braunston locks, and the kitten followed her down the tow-path waving its tail and pouncing sideways at the long still blades of grass which glittered with drops of dissolving snow. Everywhere the birds were singing, the snow was melting. The sun above was steady and strong, drawing no clouds towards it.

Emma, for the first time in six days unhampered by oilskins, swung her arms and hips and felt the blood inside her answer the strength of the sun with a vigorous movement. So, she thought, must the old singers have felt, their youth flooding back into frozen veins as they broke out with their instinctive psalms. Glory, glory, and the showering water answered 'glory' and the sturdy gates crashed together with a loud 'amen.' Never before, she thought, have I felt so able, has my body worked with such understanding of itself. And she remarked herself at every move, appraising the pull, the balance, the neat spring that evolved like a dance pattern in obedience to the tune of her mind. Never again, she thought, will I breathe so purely an air medicined with sun and country snow and sappy boughs. And between the 'never before' and the 'never again' appeared a timeless time proclaimed on every hand, with every gesture, with every still but secretly moving shadow, as: Now. Now was a crystal, sparkling as a crystal, as hard and clear and actual, prism of every colour, without subtlety as without richness but with the straight perfection of discovered beauty. Encasing it like black velvet were the walls of the world, inchoate past, uncertain presently. But Now was now, vivid with the green of microscopic moss, with the finger on steel and the wet splinter. Now was infinite. Now, thought Emma with tingling arms, was enough, enough.

The Silvers' boats, whose engine had hammered behind us all through Braunston tunnel, were still on our tails, but we kept our distance of two locks ahead. Every so often we could see the three old women knobbling about in the rear; the rattle of their descending paddles followed us down, but our lusti-ness made up for their experience and we kept our lead. However angrily Billy Silver came bicycling after us, our resolution never wavered. At every lock he arrived before we had left it and stood in the way clutching his bicycle, his face as malignant as a gargoyle's.

'I'll report you,' he said over and over again. 'It ain't right, you ought to loose us by.' Sometimes we answered him with cheerful scorn, sometimes we were silent.

'I wish we could puncture his bicycle,' said Nanette once.

'I think it might be rather mean,' said Charity, 'but we could let his tyres down and take away the pump.'

However, there was no chance of this for he clung hard on to his bicycle as though the same idea had occurred to him.

Then followed a long pound of many curves and much mud. No one was allowed to read. We steered with zealous atten-tion to the rules. Every treacherous looking bubble, every darker brown stain in the water, was avoided with crossed fingers as though it carried germs of the plague.

'We shouldn't have said it aloud, that thing about Billy Silver's bicycle,' Nanette said superstitiously. 'We're sure to pick up something in the blades or get an air-lock . . .'

At Wigrams Three a lock-keeper ran out from his house and again our trip-card was marked with the date and time of our passing. These locks were new ones, built to a more modern pattern, and from here to Birmingham all the locks were the same as these. They were certainly quicker in emptying and filling, but there was something Eastern and arid in their spaciousness and in the white-painted turrets which enclosed the paddles out of sight and leaned at an angle away from the locks, pointing up like guns blindly threatening a fixed foot of the sky. We disliked them. All the intimacy of age was gone. We missed the noisy rattle of the rickety old paddles falling. Here there was no noise, no rust. Everything was oiled and hidden. And the worst and most exhausting part of it was that each paddle needed twenty-one smooth heavy turns of the windlass to raise it, twice as many as the paddles left behind us.

Charity took advantage of the fine weather by scrubbing the butty hatches and spring-cleaning the cabin. She dragged all the fusty bedding out on to the cabin-top and beat and shook it.

'Perhaps,' she said, 'if this weather goes on our beds will dry.'

She sang the words of *Billy Boy* aloud as she worked and Nanette, catching the tune from her, shouted it into the silvery air. Charity, robbed of her little song, became pleasantly silent. She hung the scrubby strip of carpet outside and swept the floor, finding behind the stove all manner of things, like match-boxes and spoons and tooth-paste, coated with crumbs and fluff and pieces of coal, which the frequent bumpings of the butty had shaken down like acorns off a tree.

'We mustn't forget to change the batteries to-night,' said Charity, tumbling the books out of their shelf on to the side-bed and banging them free of dust. 'I'm sick of that smelly old hurricane lamp.' Nanette made no reply. 'Who are you waving to?' asked Charity, peering out past her legs.

'An aeroplane.'

A little yellow trainer plane was bumbling about uncertainly above her head.

'As if he could see you,' said Charity.

'He might. You never know. Look, he's coming back . . .'

The man in the aeroplane did see us. He swooped low down over the boats, so low we ducked our heads; rose, banked, swooped again. Nanette abandoned the tiller to Charity and leaping on top of the cabin waved the mop with wild excitement. The aeroplane fluttered its wings in salute and flew slowly away.

'We've made a friend,' cried Nanette. 'Do you think he was low enough to see our faces?'

'I'd love to fly,' said Charity vaguely, slopping water over the top of the cabin and mopping it down.

Nanette folded her arms on the tiller and leaned her chin above them. 'I wouldn't mind marrying a pilot,' she said. 'It must be much easier to go on loving a man who's always in danger.'

'If I had an aeroplane of my own,' said Charity, not bothering to listen to Nanette, 'I should never take anyone else up with me. I should just go up alone, every day, for hours and hours, and fly about in the sky on my own with no one to interfere. I say, I'm glad I scrubbed those hatches; how clean and white they look, like new wood.'

'My mother knew lots and lots of men. I can remember some of them; I always thought they were so dull. She ought to have married a pilot or an explorer, like I shall, someone she could have adored. That's the way to be faithful.'

Charity looked at her gravely. 'I wish you'd stop talking about your mother. You're always talking about her. I think she sounds a beast.'

'I can't stop thinking about her. She wasn't a beast, she was very beautiful. Sometimes I'm really quite sorry she's dead.'

All down between the ten Radford locks were ranks of rushes, and as the boats approached they bent over, servile and hissing, until their heads dabbled the water and ripples of repentance streamed to meet us. Cleopatra fell in again at the fourth lock, and as Emma leaned over to pluck the little creature out the windlass she carried in her belt slipped forward and disappeared with a splash. She threw the dripping kitten down on the path and stamped her foot.

'You stupid thing,' she said, giving it a surreptitious kick, 'I've never known such a clumsy cat. Charity,' she screamed, raising her voice to carry back to the previous lock. 'I'd like to kill your beastly cat. I hope she dies of pneumonia. I've dropped my windlass in – the Silvers are bound to catch us now.'

'I'm sorry – she's young,' cried Charity, poised far above Emma on a great slab of stone and torn by all sorts of despair; she was like a maiden deserted on a quay-side, a figure of tragedy, bright and beautiful.

'Why *will* she come lock-wheeling with me? It's not her business, I don't want her. Why don't you stop her?'

'I will, I will,' cried Charity.

We were saved by the lock-keeper, holy man in that barren land, who wheeled the last few locks for us with perfect kindness and finished by selling his windlass for two and six. Moreover he coloured our day with legend by telling us of the postman he had found drowned above the bottom lock a fortnight previously.

'I found him in the morning,' he said in his slow sing-song voice, 'before 'twas properly day. He must have been in all night, there was frost on his hair. And he was so full of whisky he was floating dead straight up, like he was walking on the bottom. I pulled him out meself, and 'twas all I could do to drag 'im.'

We asked him to hold the Silvers up if he could and he promised to do his best for us. He had a dog with him, a silky spaniel bitch, and for some reason we felt he was a lonely man, without a wife. He gave us a sprig of japonica from his garden and invited us to come and see his roses in the summer. We waved back at him as we left. He looked a singular mixture of fisherman and hunter, with his thigh-high Wellington boots, the dog at his feet, and an old checked cap pushed aside on his

101

head, but the kind scorched face he turned in our direction was the face of a friend. He chuckled and nodded after us when we waved.

In the next pound, the long Leamington pound, Charity took the motor, and Emma and Nanette had tea aboard the butty.

'Has Charity got any brothers or sisters?' asked Nanette.

'She's got one brother younger than herself, about sixteen I think. No sisters. And I think she's got a step-brother who lives in China. I suppose he's mixed up in the fighting now, but I don't really know about him.'

'She's a funny girl,' said Nanette. 'I called her a prig yesterday, but I don't think she is.'

'No, she's not a prig. She doesn't think about herself enough for that. She might *get* to being a prig later on, when she's old, but she isn't at the moment.'

'She didn't mind a bit when I called her a prig. She's a funny girl. I'd have been furious.'

'I can't imagine anyone ever would call you a prig.'

'No they wouldn't, would they?' said Nanette with interest, accepting at the same time another slice of bread and jam. 'I've been thinking about myself lately and you know, although I'm sure I'm not a prig, I don't really think I'm very nice. Isn't it awkward? Do you think it's too late to alter myself? Because if I'm not very nice, then no one very nice will ever like me. I'm afraid I'm rather shallow. What do you think?'

'Good Lord,' said Emma crossly, 'I don't know. I never think about you, why should I? And I advise you not to, either. You certainly aren't practical, and that's terribly irritating. You can't chop wood and you can't open tins, both so easy.'

'I've never had to before.'

'Well, I swear you've got to now. I'll never do it for you again. It's so dangerous to be helpless. You must train yourself.'

'The thing is,' said Nanette, absorbed in the subject and not in the least abashed, 'that I'm inclined to avoid doing things I

102

don't enjoy. And I do hate chopping wood because I'm afraid I may cut myself, and that's the reason I don't like opening tins. Can I have another slice?'

'It's your third.'

'It's my fourth.'

'You're a pig, Nanette.'

'Yes, I know I am. Which is the worse I wonder, a pig or a prig? I think on the whole I'd rather be a pig, and since I am, that's lucky.'

Immediately outside Leamington we passed by acres of allotments, the neat parcelling out of bean-sticks and cabbages on that flat and unhedged land seeming, more especially in the failing light, a very attar of depression. One or two blurred figures, grey moth-like creatures surely with every spark of passion ground out of them, bent over spades or shambled down the nondescript paths. Yet behind them flared the giant sky a citron yellow, massed with magnificent clouds which crowded together round the going sun, snatching up its dying heart to deck their black and purple edges. We passed them, these humble ghosts, like life rejecting death, and turned the bows of the *Venus* and the *Ariadne* directly into the sunset, strong but tired, tired but still triumphant, and with several more miles to go and two more locks.

It was half past seven when we tied the boats above Warwick Two and stopped the engine. Tall trees rose up beside us, their long lines interrupted by the bulges of half-born leaves. On the opposite side of the cut lay an old red-brick pub, and, although no light came from it, we heard the sounds of laughter and voices, very promising and cheerful. We primed the engine; we filled the water-cans at the tap; we chopped wood for the morning. Charity said:

'We've *got* to change the batteries.'

This horrible task was hated by us all. Charity, in the engine-hole, heaved down the newly-charged battery and pushed it out to Nanette, who lifted it, staggered a few feet

103

and bumped it heavily on top of the butty cabin while she took a breath. Then she handed it down to Emma inside the cabin, who stowed it out of sight under the side-bed, lifting out the dead one in its place to be charged again off the engine.

When it was done, Nanette said, loudly sighing: 'I wonder if we'll get muscle-bound with all this lifting and heaving, and not be able to have children.'

'What do you mean Nanette?'

Emma was coiling a rope, happy to loiter ashore in the calm primrose-smelling air of evening. Nanette swung her legs over the stern of the butty, brushing her teeth busily while she talked.

'Well, you have to be elastic, don't you, and this job must be turning our muscles into iron, especially important ones round the stomach.'

'*Will* you have children Nanette?' Charity asked from inside the cabin.

'Yes, I shall,' answered Nanette decidedly, adding punctuation with a loud spit. 'Not because I like them but because women who don't are such dry old sticks.'

'I'm bound to have them,' said Emma. 'My family always does. Why brush your teeth before supper, Nanette?'

'I'm rather worried about my teeth; they've been looking yellow lately. Charity, stop peeling those potatoes and let's all go and have a drink.'

The Silvers arrived. For one horrified moment we thought they were going to go on past us, as we had passed them the night before. But they tied up immediately ahead, their sterns to our bows, and five minutes later we were buying them beer in the pub across the water, as neighbourly and jovial as it was possible to be.

The three old ladies all wore old black hats of felt or crumpled straw, the sort of hats that grow on a head as naturally as an eyebrow above an eye. All three wore black button boots going high up round their ankles, and two of them had long black skirts with a motley of pinafores and jersies above. But the third, the one in the straw hat, wore a pair of men's blue dungarees. She looked about fifty-five, but was probably short of forty, and her apparel was even more surprising in that trousers were seldom worn by the boating women – except the very bold and young – being considered unseemly. Whether a Miss Silver or Mrs. Silver, she was the most talkative, the most masterful. We said, in this new and cordial atmosphere, that we hoped we were not holding them up.

'That's all right,' she said. 'You keep on as you are. You're doing very well. We'll all be in Brumagum to-morrow any road.'

She and Billy Silver, Nanette and some other old man with only one eye, had a game of dominoes together with plenty of beer to help them along and cackles of pleasure. The two older old ladies sat bunched tight up together in a corner, cradling their mugs in their aprons and grinning. Billy told us stories of the days when boats were horse-drawn, without motors, and had to be 'legged' through the tunnels. A plank was strapped across the boat and a man at either end of it lay down on his back and walked his feet along the side of the tunnel. He told us, and we believed him, of a friend of his who had fallen asleep halfway through, and rolling off his plank had been drowned.

'Why,' said Charity, as we groped our way back to the boats. 'They're dears. They're as nice as anything.'

'All the same,' said Emma. 'We're going to be off before them in the morning.'

'Lord, I'm tired,' said Nanette.

Our early rising seemed to be separated from us by more than the miles; already it was a different part of our lives, far behind us, forgotten like yesterday.

9

W e set the alarm for five-thirty, and at six o'clock, while
it was still dark, we crept round and untied the ropes.
With shafts we pushed the boats out from the bank and poled
them stealthily past the Silvers. Only then, with rags stuffed
down the exhaust pipe to deaden the noise, did we start the
engine. In spite of our care one of the Silvers' cabin-slides was
pushed open and Billy's head bobbed out, to stare indignantly
after us.

'Never mind,' said Emma. 'We've got at least half an hour's
start on them, probably more.'

We turned a right-angled corner and came to the foot of the
hill where the locks mounting up its side are known as Hatton
Twenty-one. At that time in the morning their full horror was
veiled to us in the semi-obscurity. Twenty-one locks, rising
immediately one after the other, were a formidable beginning
for any day. As the light grew stronger we saw their multitude
of paddles garnishing the hillside above us like the tombstones
of some exotic graveyard. All the locks were against us. We
wheeled them in turns, taking four locks each at a time. There
was one relief: the locks being so close together, boats were
taken up them strapped abreast and only a steerer on the
motor was necessary.

We had none of us washed our faces or combed our hair
that morning. After seven days afloat we were marked by an

air of negligence unknown ashore. We were very dirty. Clothes, skin and hair were dark with dirt, and smelling of various things – engine-room grease, tar, ordinary sweat, stale dampness, lockside slime. It was not a disagreeable smell, but it was strong.

A squad of soldiers marched down the main road alongside the canal, their boots sullenly in time. The sight of this orderly group of our fellow-men being marched away in another direction to an unknown destination lent a more sympathetic appearance to the locks ahead. Better a thousand locks, we felt, than that. And then we passed a wharf where witless creatures from the nearby mental home were shambling to and fro unloading coal from a canal-boat; they looked up at us, more wild than we, with vacant mouths and long arms hung idle for a moment. Their sadness dismayed us. Sadly we passed them. The sun came up clear and glittering. Spring was very near.

Presently, looking back, we saw the smoke from the Silvers' chimneys and judged that although they were so close to us in distance we were about an hour ahead of them in time. We were worried by the motor of the *Venus*. It was not running smoothly and a thin stream of black smoke came from the exhaust pipe where none should have been.

Just before nine o'clock we reached the top of the back-breaking arm-aching flight; the snubber was hauled out from the foredeck and we set off on the two and a half hour pound fringed with immensely tall trees, green pastures and budding hedges. The countryside around us was beautiful, the morning sprightly, and breakfast being by this time no more than a hollow remembrance, we made ourselves fried bacon sandwiches and drank mugfuls of the nauseating cocoa we then found so appetising. Black smoke from the exhaust pipe increased and we eyed it doubtfully.

Green and lovely, the countryside slid by on either side. Nanette finished *Good-bye to Berlin*, sighed, and turned back to Chapter One. Charity said:

'Of course you could scrub the hatches or start getting dinner ready.'

Nanette replied good-temperedly that she was too exhausted after Hatton to do anything for a few minutes except read.

The pound was uneventful: no mud interrupted us, our thoughts were mild, the sky above was spotless and pale. But as we struggled up the last five locks at Knowle we were dismayed to find the Silvers had closed in and were less than three locks behind us. We remembered the previous evening of beer and dominoes as a very brief armistice, and thought of them again, in panic, as enemies. Their little figures swarming about below us had a determined air.

'Oh hurry, hurry,' cried Nanette. 'There's something wrong with our beastly engine, I know there is, and it's getting worse.'

Charity was steering the *Venus* for the last long pound to Birmingham.

'We can't let them catch us now,' said Emma, 'Charity, don't let them catch us up, whatever you do don't loose them by. We must, we must get to Birmingham first.'

But distractedly talking, she forgot to hand Charity the noose of the snubber as the motor passed ahead out of the lock; Charity tried to snatch it, missed, and had to reverse the engine. Five minutes were lost.

'Oh HURRY,' screamed Nanette.

The black smoke was thicker, the engine was knocking. From the butty we watched with anguish the increasingly thick gout of exhaust, heard the sinister beating, cast over our shoulder more and more frequent glances, estimated the speed with which the Silvers were drawing nearer, prayed that implacable Birmingham might come half-way to meet us. Charity never turned her head. Her back was rigid, her steering a marvel of judgment. We blundered on, dying with every knot we covered. With every bridge the Silvers overhauled us. At last, unable to bear it any longer, Emma leapt off at one bridge-hole, and, racing ahead, sprang aboard the *Venus* and dived into the engine-hole. The boaters had an old trick which they called 'jamming the governor,' a trick forbidden by the company since it over-taxed and eventually ruined the engines. Remembering this, Emma pressed her finger against the governor and held it there, increasing enormously the smoke and noise, and by a very little the speed.

Foot by foot they overtook us and long before they were in ear-shot, the shouting began. Nanette was screaming back at them and forward at Charity. Emma, more than half expecting the engine to blow up, screwed her head out of the engine-hole to find that Charity, with tears streaming down her grimy face and the exhaust-smoke belching full in her wide-open eyes, was not by one inch deviating from a middle course. She held up her thumb as encouragement. Words were out of the question. The noise was deafening. The steel walls of the engine-house shook. Unless we dropped over to one side of the cut, as we undoubtedly should have done, they could hardly pass us for fear of being stuck on mud. And Charity was inflexible; she clenched the tiller-handle with white knuckles. She never once looked round.

Billy was rocketing alongside on his bicycle. 'I'll report you,' he shouted, not once but over and over again. 'You ain't fit to be on the cut, yer dirty boogers, you ain't fit to have boats, you're a disgrace, I'm going to report you.' He wobbled from side to side, his little legs spinning round, his huge mouth stretching open.

'Go and boil your head,' yelled Nanette, beside herself with muddled rage.

Dungaree-Silver was standing up on the bows of their motor-boat waving her arms and screeching like a peacock. The other two, leaving battle to their relatives, steered the boats with silent determination, like a couple of resourceful dormice.

The end was bound to come. The Silvers' motor-boat, losing patience, crowded up alongside the *Ariadne*, risking whatever mud there might be. The crone on the bows shook her fist right under Nanette's nose and Nanette let out a terrible scream of defeat. Charity heard it and turned her head for the first time. Seeing that it was now too late for defiance, she at once switched the engine low and waved them ahead. Immediately, the noise subsided. Everyone stopped shouting. The hideous clatter of the *Venus'* engine ceased. In comparative silence the other boats edged by us, the two old women steering them staring straight ahead unblinkingly as they passed. The one in dungarees was also mute, her flood of words exhausted; her eyes, from intense enjoyment, gleamed a bright and happy brown. On the tow-path, Billy rested himself and rubbed his sweating face with his arm. Emma leaned out of the engine hole, sorrowing. We were beaten half an hour from Birmingham.

Charity gazed after their dwindling sterns.

'Rot them,' she said, very loudly. Then she blew her nose and began to pick the soot from the corners of her eyes.

We crawled on, the engine more dead than alive, and on reaching Tysley Wharf found the Silvers, who had shrewdly unclothed their butty in the long pound, already tied up under a crane and beginning to be unloaded.

'There goes our turn,' said Nanette morosely, 'I wonder what on earth's wrong with our engine. . . .'

'Got something round your prop, ain't you, mate?' shouted a loafer as we crept down the wharf-side looking for a gap in which to tie ourselves.

We had plenty round our prop. We could feel with a shaft a quelching mass of rubbish clinging out of sight beneath the *Venus*.

'Rope,' said Emma, hauling out a few tell-tale strands.

'Rags,' she added, unhooking a coloured scrap from the shaft, 'and – my God – I believe we've got a tyre there too.'

111

A fragment of red rubber was spiked on the hook of the shaft.

One of the unloaders came along to help us, and took a turn at poking. 'You ain't 'arf got yourself something proper down there,' he said, splashing away. 'There's wire too, I wouldn't be surprised, that's what's holding it all together so tight. Wonder the old boat went at all.'

'We couldn't have picked all that up,' said Emma, aghast. 'The Silvers must have put it there. I bet the Silvers put it there. They planted it last night, I bet they did, when we were all tied up together at Warwick.'

Whether they did or not was beyond proving, but they hung over their hatches very complacently while we struggled, and offered friendly advice. Even with help it took us an hour to clear the propeller shaft, and the stuff we got out was astonishing. Wire there certainly was, and the inner tube of a bicycle tyre, innumerable rags, what seemed to be an almost undamaged cardigan, ends of rope and a sack.

There were several other pair of boats tied up besides the Silvers and our own, and traffic was constantly passing, setting us all awash – chiefly single horse-drawn boats loaded with coal, smacking along at a great rate. For a view we had factory chimneys and dumps of rusty iron, the tin roofing of sheds and the blackened stones of warehouses. It was strange to remember that only half a mile away we had passed under an arch of trees and between steep bushy banks. Farther down, a boat was being unloaded of a cargo of boots. Every few seconds a lorry dashed into the yard, was loaded up with steel billets, or boots, or whatever it might be, had its weight noted down by the clerk scribbling in an office at the back, and tore away again in a cloud of dust.

Between the piles of steel were strewn odd lumps of wood used by empty boats for ballast, and the usual scrap assortment that collects in such a place: pieces of wire, rusty files, nails, grease rags, and lengths of rope too rotten for any use.

The boaters' wives stretched their lines from billet to paling and hung out tattered washing to catch the breeze. Their lean, hungry watch-dogs prowled about with pricked ears, sniffing for food and finding only uneatable bed-springs and empty cans. The children either dawdled round the boats watching their dads at work, or played wise games with bits of broken chain. A lumbering noise from the several cranes rose above all other noises, and the voices of the men shouting: 'Down a bit Bert . . . take it away.' Unlike Limehouse, where the walls of the pool had towered over us, this wharf lay on a level with the boats and the whole scene was therefore more domestic.

This was the time when boats were cleaned. Newly-scrubbed drawers lay drying on the side. The hatches were scrubbed, the floors were scrubbed, the step of the butty cabin, a movable block of wood, was scrubbed, the cotton-line decorating the helms in various plaits and patterns was scrubbed to a frosty whiteness. The women excelled at scrubbing; they scrubbed like demons. And the deep frown graven between their eyes by sun and winter wind, made their application even fiercer, like a furious vengeance. We had already learnt that their harsh expressions could be misleading – they were not all the viragos they looked.

When the scrubbing was done, they turned to their polishing. They polished the brass on the engine-house roof, the brass rings round their chimneys, the brass round the portholes, the infinite number of brass knobs and horse-brasses hanging inside the cabins, and whatever other odd strips of brass their husbands had freakishly nailed on for extra adornment. When the polishing was done, they washed their garments and their lace curtains. When the washing was pegged up, they went shopping, returning from these ventures with drooping string bags and the fury on their faces unabated.

Either they were very clean indeed, and their boats shone and sparkled and gleamed in the mild sunshine, as these round us did, or they were incredibly dirty, and had the word 'dirty' prefixed permanently to their names by their scornful fellows: the Dirty Hoppers littered the cut with their dirty children and were cousins of the Dirty Finns.

There were always seven children in the Hopper family: each year the eldest child died, and each year another was born to replace it. Or perhaps when each year a child was born the eldest had to die to give it room. Or perhaps we were wrong altogether, but so it appeared to us. The babies all had milky fair hair dulled by dirt and neglect and clotted into spikes over their verminous little heads. Their father had sores round his mouth and his children inherited them. The older ones wore men's trousers cut off unevenly to show their thin purple ankles, and from under the swamping brims of second-hand caps they looked out with the sharp intelligent eyes of birds. No brass was ever polished aboard those boats. No roses were painted on the water-cans. Dirty they were called, and dirty almost beyond belief they were.

We fetched the letters waiting for us at the office and read them avidly.

'My sister went to a dance last week,' said Emma. 'Doesn't it seem funny. I've almost forgotten what it's like to dance.'

'Oh listen,' cried Nanette, 'how awful. My aunt's been given a medal by the Foreign Office for twenty years service without being late or absent once. Think of it! What a ghastly record.'

'Fancy having an aunt in the Foreign Office,' said Charity. 'Why not?'

'I don't know. It sounds odd. An aunt . . . and the Foreign Office . . .'

'She is odd: dull-odd. But awfully clever.'

We were standing reading the letters half-way across the yard between the office and our boats.

'Come on,' said Nanette suddenly, stuffing her letters into a trouser pocket. 'I'm sick of all this. Let's go and have a bath.'

'Bert,' we said to the crane-driver. 'When do you think we'll get unloaded?'

Bert looked at his watch. 'Not to-day,' he said.

We took a tram to the nearest public baths and paid nine-pence each for the best and biggest bath possible to buy. After our usual close quarters it was like being in a palace. Shining white tiles surrounded us, lofty ceilings. The bath-attendant gave us each a towel and a small cake of soap and led us to three adjoining cubicles. Here she unlocked the taps and filled the mammoth baths high with steamy water. Then she left us. We stripped our filthy garments off and wallowed up to our necks. It was marvellous; it was our anticipated dream.

'Hi!' shouted Emma.

'What's the matter?'

'There was a man looking at me through the window.'

Almost at once Charity cried out: 'You beast – go away;' this was followed by a crash as she flung her nail-brush at the window, and then the splosh of her sponge.

'I've got my finger on the bell – why doesn't someone come,' shouted Emma. Charity had climbed on a chair and was craning her neck out of the high window.

'I'll fetch the police,' she cried. Except for some laurel-bushes, the path outside appeared to be empty.

'Did he look in at you, Nanette?'

'I don't know,' said Nanette, 'I rolled on to my stomach. I don't mind if he did see my back. Anyway, the water's so dirty I don't think he could.'

In each bath the water was a deep brown colour with a scum of filth slopping about on the surface. When we pulled the plugs out it rushed away down the drain in a second, leaving behind a thick coating of dirt. Ashamed of our dregs, we hurried on our smelly clothes and left in haste. On the way out Emma stopped at the office.

'There was a man,' she said, putting her mouth against the glass slit, 'looking in at us through the windows.'

The ticket-girl was eating a bun and drinking tea. She slewed her chair round.

'Oh, they're awful,' she said. 'They're always doing that.'

'I rang the bell. I kept my finger on it for about two minutes; didn't you hear?'

'They're out of order,' said the girl. 'We're always having complaints.'

'It's not nice,' Charity said severely, 'to be looked at while you're bathing.'

'No,' she agreed. 'It isn't right. It's being so close to the road and that. You just can't stop them.'

We went down the steps and into the chilly air of late afternoon. Nanette said:

'Well, at least I don't feel so itchy, but I'm awfully hungry. Let's buy some food.'

So we bought apples and buns and wandered in Birmingham's uncharming streets eating them.

'I've never seen a town,' said Charity, 'so full of ugly people. Aren't they all hideous?'

It was the greatest pleasure to be ashore, critical, free, and with the rest of the day our own. We climbed on the first bus that passed and rode towards the centre of the city. Nanette fell into conversation with a sailor. Charity and Emma, sitting behind, heard him say:

'It may seem funny, but I can't swim a stroke.'

'Then what do you do when you're shipwrecked?' asked Nanette in her pertinent way.

'I drops down to the bottom,' he said, 'and runs like hell for shore.' Nanette said afterwards she liked his curly hair.

'What an extraordinary place it is,' said Charity as we strolled down a darkening street. 'Full of enormous new red-brick pubs on the one hand, and posters on the other saying, "Drink is Sin". And so frantically municipal – look, even the studs in the road have got "B.C." stamped across them. If I were as ugly as Birmingham I wouldn't be so proud of myself, would you?'

We had finished the buns some time before but being still hungry bought ourselves a quantity of fish and chips and munched them on the pavement. As we ate we realized slowly that the name of our destination had become a town and we were standing in it. We had arrived. We were there. Though defeated by the Silvers, still we had in a certain measure triumphed: it was a fact that we had brought our boats from London to Birmingham, and to celebrate this we went to a cinema.

They were showing the film, *Of Mice and Men*. For two hours we forgot Birmingham, the cut, even ourselves. It was cold when we came out, frosty and clear-starred. We were silent during the long bus-ride out to Tysley, saturated with sleep and pleasure.

'My, what a film,' said Charity once.

'I do like sitting in a cinema,' said Nanette. 'The seats are so comfortable, and it's warm, it's wonderful.'

The bus, except for ourselves, was empty. We sat on the top in front and stretched out our legs. Nanette was very tired; she lolled her head sideways, half asleep. Charity stared ahead, patient as a Madonna, and Emma dug her hands deep down in her pockets for warmth.

'It's nice,' she said, 'to think that no one, none of my family, no one at all, knows exactly where I am at this moment. I'm absolutely private from everyone.'

'Except us,' said Charity dreamily, 'and we don't care a pin about one another really. Of course we're meant to be friends. People think of us as friends. They say: "those three girls, they get on so *well* together" – which we do of course – "they're so *fond* of each other". But that's not true, we're not a bit. We aren't really friends. You wouldn't die to save my life, and I'm quite sure I shouldn't die for either of you.'

'Oh Charity, how silly – as though that's anything to do with it.'

'I'm a very good friend of yours,' said Nanette drowsily, 'so stop grumbling and shut up.'

'Oh we like each other well enough, but what's the use of that, what *power* is there in liking? Feelings don't count unless they give you courage.'

'Charity, shut UP. You go against my grain. You ought to be burning at a stake, not working on a canal.'

We were all silent again. The bus jolted onwards.

'Had a nice time, girls?' said the night watchman on Tysley Wharf. We dallied for a few moments to talk. He was a big hairy man who had once served in the Royal Fusiliers. We leaned in at the doorway of his hut, irresistibly drawn by the fire and the bright electric light.

'Doesn't it hurt to be tattooed?' asked Nanette, who was always curious about other people's pain.

'No,' he said, 'you don't hardly feel it. Some does, mind. It depends if you got a tender skin. I ain't.' He unbuttoned the front of his shirt to show us his chest. On it was tattooed a large tombstone with flowers twined round it and an angel blowing a trumpet above it and on it the words: 'In Memory of Mum and Dad.' Over it, like moss, flourished the gingery hair.

'I never understand how ladies manage,' he said.

'*Ladies*. . . .?' cried Nanette.

'Wot, ain't you ever seen a tattooed lady?'

'No, *never*.'

'I had a pal,' he said, 'when I was in the Army, with a battleship across his chest. Right across his chest it was, from one side to t'other. We was in a pub together one night, Arthur and me, and there was a young lady there taking particular notice of Arthur, kep' looking at him and looking at him till at last he says, "Ullo" he says, "you'll know me next time." "No offence," she says, "I was just noticing your battleship" she says – it was a warm night – "an' thinking you and me ought to get together sometime." "Why what d'you mean?" says Arthur, feeling his way. So with that she opens up as well, and would you believe it, she had roses tattooed all over her breasts.'

We wriggled shyly.

'And more than that,' said the night-watchman, 'Arthur and her was very drawn together, and he went off with her, just like she said, and was gone a week. And he told me after, he couldn't hardly put his finger on an inch of her without there was a picture. She worked in a fair and was doing very nicely I believe. But Arthur didn't half get in trouble with the Army when he come back.'

'Ain't you ever seen a tattooed lady?' crooned Nanette as we rollicked away to the boats. It was eleven o'clock and the dogs were growling at us.

10

We were awakened by a thunderous knocking on the side of the butty. The alarm had not been set: it was eight o'clock. Woefully unprepared we sprang out of bed and began shuffling into our clothes. The banging was repeated with obvious anger.

'All right, all right, coming.'

'We want to unload you and the boats ain't ready. The gang's waiting.' The foreman, with whom we were usually on the best of terms, was thoroughly vexed. Sluggards, he thought us, and worse. We burst out of the cabins with buttons undone and boots unlaced. Three minutes before, we had been fast asleep.

'We forgot to set the alarm. Terribly sorry, we won't be long . . .'

There was no excuse. All around us the day was well ahead. The sun was miles up, chimneys were smoking, babies were squalling, washing flapped abroad. The men on the wharfside, kicking their boots and waiting for us to uncloth the boats, had all had their breakfasts an hour or more before, had risen in the dark and queued perhaps for trams in cold streets still full of shadow. Eight o'clock was a late hour. We scrambled about on the butty, tearing untied the top-strings and bundling back the tarpaulin that for six days had kept hidden our cargo of steel. Out came the planks, the stands, the wooden supports, and were flung ashore. With side-cloths unrolled and an air of slovenly haste predominant, we raised our crimson faces and said:

'There you are . . . .'

At once two men leapt into the hold, the crane swung into position and the unloading of the *Ariadne* began.

More calmly we began to uncloth the *Venus*, folding the topcloths neatly and stowing them away under the cratch, rolling down the side-cloths and lashing them in two tight pipe-lines along the gunwales. The weather was lovely, not still, as the previous day had been, but with a brisk breeze whipping the dirty water into a semblance of purity. The labour of Limehouse was very soon undone and the *Venus* lay trimly open to the sky.

'You've took in a bit of water, ain'tcher?' said one of the unloaders.

We leaned our chins on the tarry gunwale and looked over into the *Ariadne's* hold. Water in the stern end was swaying about above the floor-boards and the men trampled through it as they worked.

'Lord,' said Charity. 'We ought to bale that – your feet must be getting soaked.'

'Ah, leave it alone now,' said the man. 'It don't hurt our boots and it'll help to keep the boat down once she's empty.'

It was a gymnastic sort of day. We enjoyed swinging ourselves up on to the cross-beams and the other athletic feats necessary in unclothing a boat. But gymnastics make for hunger, especially before breakfast, and Charity, catching a particular glance from Nanette, disappeared into the butty cabin and soon there was the smell of bacon frying. Breakfast we ate at nine o'clock, leaving the back-door of the butty open so that we could see into the hold and keep an eye on affairs there. Charity made out a shopping list while she drank her tea. The boat rocked from side to side as the billets were taken out of her.

122

'Bread,' said Charity. 'And I'll see if I can get some fresh milk. Potatoes. Something green in vegetables, like cauliflower. Ink. Fish perhaps. Prunes, because they're so good for us.'

'Horrid,' said Nanette. 'Get sultanas instead.'

'Cigarettes,' said Emma.

'And matches. We all ought to put another pound in the kitty – there's only ten bob left.'

'Buy a newspaper,' shouted Nanette after her as she left. 'Do you think she heard? She'll probably buy *The Times* and I meant the *Mirror*.'

'Don't be so hard on her,' said Emma.

'I'm not hard on her; I'm hard on myself.' Enjoying a mood of virtue, she added: 'And now I'm going to chop some firewood.'

Emma went off to the engine-room to clean the mud-box, but almost at once was called away by the gang. The *Ariadne* was empty and they needed to have the boats swapped round. Nanette, crouching down on the wharf with a chopper in her hand and several rotten planks beside her, was being closely watched by a small boy called Amos from one of the neighbouring boats. She threw down the chopper immediately. We untied the boats, withdrew the *Ariadne*, now as light as a cockle, pulled the *Venus* in against the wharf and taking the butty-boat outside her again lashed them both abreast. Nanette picked up her chopper and Emma went back to her mud-box.

The mud-box held a filter through which the circulating water passed before cooling the engine, and was placed under one of the steel floor-boards in the most awkward corner. She bent herself over it, scraping her hands and knocking her head. The nuts were stiff and there was not sufficient room to turn the spanner. She wrestled and swore, and had presently skinned the knuckles of her left hand and was swearing harder. The mud-box, once the lid had been taken off it, was unsavoury, full almost to the brim with a very soft mud compounded of all sorts of things it was pleasanter to leave nameless. She scooped it into a bucket with her hands and rinsed it back into its native canal. Having screwed on the lid, she discovered the filter lying behind her on the floor and the spanner had to be gingerly employed again. Her upsidedown head sang with blood. Her knees were creaking. She wiped her face and left a smear of black oil across it from mouth to ear. The engine itself was very dirty and due for a polish. Emma went back to the butty cabin to fetch some clean rags.

Nanette was sitting on a pile of steel watching Amos chop the wood.

'I thought . . .' began Emma.

'Yes, I know,' replied Nanette placidly, 'I gave him sixpence. It made him very happy. Don't be grudging.'

'What are you looking so black in the face about?' said Amos, borrowing from his parents' store of traditional wit.

Emma absently rubbed the smear on her cheek with one sleeve, forgetting to smile. 'How old are you?' she asked.

'Dunno,' answered Amos, splitting wood with a deft hand, for he was showing-off to Nanette. He was the size of an eight-year-old, but we guessed him to be about twelve. When he walked it was with a marked swagger, and he would later be a terror with the girls, his name on all the lock-beams from London to Birmingham.

'Which are your boats?'

He nodded his head backwards laconically. 'You don't want to tie your side-strings like that,' he said. He showed us a different sort of hitch and made us practise it until we had it right. We thanked him. Again he inclined his head with a winning mixture of the lord and ape, and went back to chopping wood at Nanette's feet. Emma, with a handful of rags and a tin of Bluebell metal polish, returned to the engine-room.

She started with the brass, picking out the brass cocks and handles and the brass feed-pipes, and when they were winking

124

at her like so many eyes, began the greater task of clearing grease from the body of the engine and rubbing up the green and red enamel paint. The engine-hole familiarized itself minutely to her eye as she worked, until its character and her own became fused and her erratic train of thought arose directly out of this fusion, incorporating in all seriousness the oddest details of screws and piping with faces and conversations. Afterwards, whenever she met certain people the smell of the engine-hole came back to her, and certain ideas were confused for ever in her mind with winking brass cocks and green paint. She sat inside on the tool-box with her hands polishing and her thoughts wandering for twenty minutes, and when she came out Charity, hung with shopping-bags, was talking to Nanette. Two bottles of milk stood beside the pile of firewood.

'What funny bottles of milk.' They were the kind that usually hold lemonade, with ginger-pop lids.

'It's pasteurized milk,' said Charity. 'I think it means they've cooked it to kill the bugs.'

We each had a mug of it there and then and found it delicious, creamy, with a faintly burnt taste. We had a little more.

'Where's Amos?' asked Emma.

'He's going to mend our slow puncture for us. He's gone to get his outfit. And look, he's sold me three brass rings for the chimney.' Nanette was aggressively pleased with herself.

'How much?'

'Never mind. Much too much I know, but that's my affair. They're for my chimney and I'm going to get the blacksmith back at the depot to fix them on – Amos says he will.'

'And look,' cried Charity, diving her hand into a bag. 'I've bought us a brass chain for the water can. So much smarter than that shabby bit of string, and stronger too.'

'Brass, brass,' said Emma peevishly. 'It only means more work.'

'One minute, two minutes every day – the boats aren't properly boats till we get some brass on them. And if Nanette has rings on the *Venus* we'll have to have rings on the butty-chimney too.'

'Soon you'll want lace in the cabins and plates. It takes all our time and strength to keep the boats going, you know it does. We aren't proper boaters. It seems to me silly to copy them so.'

'If you feel like that, why don't you give up boating and go into the A.T.S.?' said Nanette with unusual snappiness, guilty on the firewood score. We hung on the brink of a row. Charity, who was bored by quarrels, melted into the cabin with her shopping. Then Amos came lurching up with his puncture outfit, and the echo of a nursery code of unity in front of strangers saved us from any further sharp words.

Almost immediately the *Venus* was emptied of her last load of billets and her bows had risen up out of the water as high as the butty-boat. We spent half an hour in sweeping clear the holds of the two boats, choking our throats with ochre-coloured dust in the process and tossing ashore fragments of ballast and other flotsam. Several of the floor-boards had been smashed either in careless loading or unloading. We taxed the men, now busy in another pair of boats, with this crime, and they hotly denied having anything to do with it. As we stood watching them load aluminium one disc of it slipped out of the sling and disappeared between boat and wharf with a greasy splash. We glanced instinctively up towards the crane-driver. With mock dismay he rolled his eyes, then, broadly grinning, laid one finger on his lips. The men in the boat blew their noses between their fingers and afterwards glossed them up on their sleeves. They also spat and avoided our eyes.

'Of course it was them that bust our floor-boards,' said Charity as we walked away. 'They don't care a bit, but I do. When we load coal at Coventry it'll all trickle through into the

126

bilges, and then after the coal's been taken out we'll have to lift up the floor-boards and clean those slimy, stinky, beastly bilges, and there's nothing I hate more.'

'Except changing batteries,' said Nanette.

'Except the Bottom Road,' said Emma, making shadowy every other horror by mentioning the horror supreme, a punishment for nothing which awaited us that very afternoon.

The Bottom Road was the old-fashioned canal that linked Coventry and Birmingham. It was largely used by single horse-drawn boats running a day's journey one way or the other, local carriers of coal, and each lock was the width of only one boat. Previously, our kind of boats, running in pairs, had retraced their way back as far as Braunston and there branched off to Coventry, but this route was now considered wasteful, and so instead of turning the boats round at Tysley, we were being sent straight on, past the shunting-yards and back-street grime of Birmingham, to battle for two days with that unholy of all unholies, the Bottom Road.

We had had one first-hand experience under the guidance of Tilly, but apart from that had learned much about it with increased misgivings, for there was no one on the cut who had not at one time or another suffered from the Bottom Road. To begin with, the butty had to be lugged by hand and sweat down the short pounds from lock to lock, and in the long pounds, undredged for years, more things than mud lay hidden: gravelbanks lurked there, bricks, and even in one place, it was sworn, an old plough which had tumbled in years before and been left alone to rust under the water, a death-trap to boats; more Dunlop tyres floated there submerged, like unattached mines and nearly as dangerous, than in the whole length between London and Brum. Each story was capped with a worse. The Bottom Road was a fable of disaster. We set out towards it just before lunch, as uneasy as it was possible to be, and by the time we reached its other end we had our own quota of stories to add to the common saga.

Amos, who fancied himself our closest friend, rode with us as far as the first lock. He had mended the slow puncture in the front tyre of our bicycle and replaced it with several quick ones, as we were later to discover. We asked if he had seen the Blossoms and found we had missed them by only a few hours. They had left Tysley Wharf at sun-up the previous morning. Nanette was full of grief.

'We'll never see them now,' she lamented.

'Yes, we shall. We'll meet them I should think just outside London on their way back to Birmingham.'

'What's the use of that?' cried Nanette. 'We can only wave to them. I don't see how you can keep up a friendship with anyone on a canal when all you can do is wave to them once a fortnight.'

'We'll save money on the beer we don't buy them,' said Emma judiciously.

We were passing as she spoke the wharf where the Guinness was unloaded, and Amos took a lift back on a pair of fly-boats just starting South.

'We'll be after you,' he shouted, no doubt meaning to comfort us for the loss of his company.

'And pass us too I expect,' muttered Emma. The Bottom Road had cast a gloom on all our spirits.

Surely no locks in England were as dirty as the flight at which we now arrived. The tow-path looked and felt as though it had been laid with wet soot and the dung dropped plentifully on it by the many passing horses was no improvement. The lock walls were covered, not with that green slime natural to age and water, but with a black oily substance, as thick as treacle. Beams, paddles, everything we touched or tried not to touch, was coated with this same sticky dirt. Every now and then we passed through belts of darkness, under the girders of a railway or a main road, when the lock beneath was colder and more shadowy, and we heard trains or buses thundering above our heads. The factories we passed were squalid affairs with blackish bricks and smothered glass. They crouched beside that disenchanted water like old slum women nourished on gin and disease.

No towing was allowed down these locks. It was against the rule for two boats going the same way to be in one of the short pounds at the same time. We thought it a hard rule, and chafed against it; but this part of the canal was not owned by the Grand Union – we were only visitors, and not very welcome visitors, and we had to be on our best behaviour. So Charity took the motor on in front and was lost to us for an hour.

Having no lock-wheeler, she steered the *Venus* gently up to the closed gates of each lock and left her there with the engine ticking ahead to keep her from floating away, while she made ready the lock. Alone she had to wind up and drop the paddles, beware of the sill, take the boat back a few feet, forward a few feet, shut and open the gates, springing up and down between the *Venus* and the lock-side several times during each operation, and unavoidably spreading the black dirt over the palms of her hands, the front of her jersey, her trousers and her boots, as she did so. We caught a glimpse now and again of her blue figure flashing ahead in the monochromatic distance, like the kingfisher on Tring Summit.

If Charity dirtied herself handling the *Venus*, we were hardly cleaner as we tramped sourly in her rear with the helpless *Ariadne*. To the butty mast was tied a very long cotton-line, replica of the one bought and lost at Fenny Stratford. One of us chaperoned the *Ariadne* through each lock; the other ran ahead to wheel the next one, and then, hurrying back, harnessed herself to the end of the cotton-line and tugged the butty down the short pound, wishing it were shorter. Someone had to stay aboard in order to steer her, and we took it turn and turn about. Twice we met a horse-boat, the horse dashing along at double the speed of its human counterpart and this in spite of having to drag a boat loaded down to the gunwales with coal. The little boys aboard them, steering, had faces and clothes to match their cargoes. Each time the boatman stopped his horse on meeting us, and, letting his cotton-line go slack in the water, allowed our butty-boat to float across it.

The speed at which these horse-boats moved lent them an air of important haste that made us, in comparison, seem aimless and clumsy. We never overcame an apologetic feeling of trespass when we met them, for though we hated their canal, it was their canal, not ours. We found them not a talkative breed of people, though equally not unfriendly, born and raised in the district, respectable and hard-working, with Sunday a day of rest.

Charity, when she reached the bottom of the flight, tied up the *Venus* and came back to help us. The cotton-line, which had been new and snowy-white when we started, had by now been dropped many times on the tow-path and dragged in the filth. Picking it up, we picked up as well the grime and grit it had gathered, and winding it round our waists or shoulders for better purchase, had to force ourselves to be indifferent to what it lavishly rubbed off on our clothes. Our flesh was bitten into by its wet strictness, our backs were soon aching. Nanette tore a gash on her left hand with a nail and was surprisingly hardy about it, refusing to bind it up till later and only saying, as she licked off the blood and dirt:

'I wonder if it'll go bad. That nail was rusty.'

There was one consolation, the consolation of all empties: in the long pounds the butty was tied close up to the motor and there was no longer the need of jumping off at bridge-holes and racing ahead in order to relieve the steerer of the *Venus*. From the fore-deck of the *Ariadne* it was an easy jump down on to the deck of the motor-boat, with the tiller-handle as a support, and an easy enough scramble back the other way, so that food, conversation and company could flow easily between the boats and the family feeling was strengthened.

There was no time for us now to have a proper meal; instead, we blunted our appetites on bread and cheese, promising ourselves a feast of fish and chips for supper in compensation.

In ten minutes we had arrived at the second flight. Emma was sent ahead with the *Venus* into exile. Nanette and Charity distastefully tangled themselves in the cotton-line, and the descent went on.

Birmingham was still beside us. Birmingham trams still whined in the distance, Birmingham bridges still crowded over us, tattered hoardings rose above the stumps of chimneys, tin advertisements in chrome-yellow and South Sea Island blue of starch and tea and rupture appliances were nailed to the mouldy brickwork. At one lock three little children came down from the road and stood in a row watching Nanette and Charity. Strung out from hand to hand, with swollen ears and dribbling noses, silent, with faces colourless except where the thin blood had been stung to protest by the pinch of cold, they had nothing in common with the brats who had tortured us in London. One of them whispered to Nanette as she trotted past them.

'What?' she said, not unkindly but loudly through habit. They shrank away, withered with fear. Nanette wound a paddle and came back to them.

'What did you say to me?'

Eyes as unsullied as tears looked up at her. Neither the scabs nor the soft smeary mouth nor the rags nor the great boots could obliterate the natural jewel. Childhood that was given nothing but its breath and its weakness confronted her, childhood that had everything to shrink from and nothing to hold to, except a smaller hand, and nothing to ask except:

'Will you give us a ride, miss?'

She lifted them up one by one and handed them down to Charity, who put them in the empty hold and told them to be good. She gave them Cleopatra to play with, but cats were

131

common where they came from and probably spat, for they made no effort to touch her. When the boat bumped at the next lock the smallest one fell over, dragging the other two down as well and there they stayed, clumped together on the floor-boards at the bottom of the hold with their brittle little legs stuck out before them, being good, as they always were – that is to say: silent, without laughing; fearful, without crying; quite still except for their eyes turning, and for security close together.

Charity stuffed their pockets with oranges and lifted them out at the last lock, alternately frowning to herself and smiling at them.

'Good-bye,' she said affectionately.

'Good-bye,' they answered, the whisper going obediently from mouth to mouth like a ripple impelled to break against the shore. Together, hand in hand, they trudged up the tow-path to the road.

'I wish they'd thrown stones at us,' said Charity, angrily pushing ahead the accelerator. 'Are they children? They frighten me.' And the frown on her face remained for as long as she went on thinking of all the other children she knew, well-fed, with tweed overcoats from Bond Street and manners from the family tree.

Then came a narrow neck of water with an office standing beside it, and here a man ran out and again our trip-card was marked. It was by now a battered piece of cardboard, disfigured by mud and frayed at the corners, but the stains were honourable and the different times and dates scrawled down it in ink and pencil made it a document of human struggle. Half of it was still blank. Charity crammed it back in the drawer where it lived and said:

'You know, we haven't posted any of our "North Bound" cards. I'd forgotten them, hadn't you?'

Beside the cut, at various locks, were boxes into which we were meant to drop one of these cards as we passed as an additional check on the boats travelling up and down. Usually we forgot and found at the end of every trip the drawer still full of blue and pink squares which we used instead as shopping lists or postcards or for drawings.

Immediately after the office was a hairpin bend. We got ourselves round it somehow, disregarding the usual spate of contradictory advice shouted out to us by men ashore, and turned at last away from Birmingham towards the flat country that lay between us and Coventry. A fresh breeze blew into our mouths and shook our lustreless hair.

Nanette flopped down on the motor-deck beside Charity, who, because of the noise from the engine, had not heard her coming and started violently.

'It's about tying up. Either we tie up at the Pictures early, or else we go on to the *Black Dog*, which means I can't remember how many more locks. What do you say?'

'What does Emma say? And I wish you'd make a noise before you jump down, it startles me.'

'She says she doesn't mind and leaves it to us to decide. It would be rather nice to tie up early and see a film.'

'Well, I don't know; the *Venus* is running a treat and we've finished the dirty locks, the others aren't nearly so bad. I feel really we ought to push on while we can. We can never be certain when we're going to be held up for, well, you know – trouble.' It was a word we hardly dared to mention.

'I don't mind really. I like the *Black Dog* and the weather's nice and there's no one shoving behind us.'

'I'm not sure about this wind,' said Charity, sniffing it as though it carried a smell of danger. 'It's getting stronger.'

'Not really – it's only because we're clear of the town. All right, I'll tell her *Black Dog* then, shall I?'

No plans are safe when you travel on a canal. We agreed to tie at the *Black Dog*, and no sooner had we agreed than it became impossible. Nanette, on her way up to the bows of the

133

Venus with a rope, stopped short outside the engine-hole with a cry of horror.

'What is it?' shouted Charity.

Nanette threw down the rope and hurried back. 'The engine-room's *black* – the fly-wheel's in the bilges. It's made the most awful mess – go and look.'

The water, which when the *Venus* was loaded had been evenly distributed along the whole length of her bilges, had run back into the engine-room when the cargo was taken out and raised the level there by several inches. The fly-wheel, revolving in it, flung out a spray of oil-black water. The ceiling dripped it; the steel floor-boards were covered; it ran down the walls; it spattered in Charity's face as she bent to look inside. Brass cocks and green paint, Emma's morning toil, were lost under a liquid black pall.

Charity dropped into the heart of this unsalubrious rain and kicked on the bilges pump. It jerked up and down once or twice and then stopped. Something was choking it. She climbed out, her face freckled with oil, and said to Nanette:

'We'll have to tie up at the Pictures after all – the pump won't work.'

The scrap-yard, where half an hour later we tied, belonged to a suburb as characterless as all such suburbs of big towns, consisting of a great number of newly and badly built houses, very pretentious in their gabling and unpretentious in the people who lived there, with a red-brick public-house and a cinema as the dominating factors, and no sign of a church. Only the road bounding through it was made wide and strong to carry the constant stream of lorries and Army convoys. Unimaginative cleanliness, the respectable password to success, marked the district with its sad order: saffron-dyed netting veiled the windows; the new shops had their signs in chromium-plating; the square of grass identical to the front of each house, was neatly clipped. It was because of the cinema, standing exactly opposite to where we tied, that this stopping-place was called on the cut 'the Pictures.'

Charity unscrewed the bottle-shaped top of the pump and delved inside for the two valves. These she wiped clean, and then, with vaseline smeared on the end of a rod, fished about in the dark hole for what she could find. Out came the rod studded with lumps of coal and grit and fragments of wood. She repeated this cleansing operation several times and then replaced the valves and screwed on the top.

'Now we'll have to start the engine,' she said. 'Stand clear.'

We started the engine and leaned outside to see what happened. The circulating water was plopping vigorously out from one hole, and presently from another hole farther up crept out a dirty trickle, increasing with every beat of the engine to a strong and stronger jet, until it was spouting clear, as rhythmically as the strokes of a heart.

'Hurray,' cried Charity. 'It's working.'

The fly-wheel, in the meantime, was broadcasting over everything, including our backs, a shower of oily water. We scrambled out and looked at one another glumly.

'To think we had a bath yesterday.'

'To think I cleaned that flaming engine this morning.'

As soon as the water-level had dropped below the fly-wheel we set to work with rags to clear away as much of the filth as we could. The rags, when sodden, we flung into the scrap-yard, which was careless of us and what everybody did, for the wind would first dry them and then blow them into the canal, from where they would be rescued at some cost by our propeller blades on the next trip, and throwing them ashore again we would curse everyone but ourselves; and the wind would dry them and blow them, and so it went on.

'The floor and the ceiling can stay as they are,' said Nanette at last. 'I've done enough. What a *bugger*.' This, pronounced in her high friendly voice, with a strain of indignation in it, made us both laugh.

135

'You may laugh,' she said, smelling her hands with a wry face, 'but just think how we'll have to wash to-night, all over, and the time it'll take. I'm too cross to go to the pictures. I only want to eat.'

The fish and chip shop had a notice outside it saying in chalk: 'No frying to-day.' It had been a bad day, and dirty, with a bad ending. That night, before going to bed, Charity stood outside in the *Ariadne's* hatches and looked at the sky. The wind smarted her face, still damp from a sponge, and made the legs of her pyjamas gutter like candle-flames. Above her the stars were bright and single, but clouds racing up from the north threatened with long smoky fingers to blot them out.

Aloud she said: 'The wind's awfully strong. I hope it doesn't rise any more in the night.'

She said it as a prayer, and almost at once the stars plunged out of sight, and the hatches' doors slammed shut, and the two boats shook themselves and rubbed together uneasily.

11

We awoke to the racketing of a gale, and by gale our day was distinguished. There were no hills to break its fury. The wind tore straight across flat fields and caught us broadside on. The boats, poor empty shells, staggered against the bank and there were pinned as helpless as butterflies on a board. Again and again we shafted them out and whipped the engine up to its full speed. Again and yet again they disobeyed us and obeyed the cruder strength that bore down on them across the thorny hedges. By inches, by feet we struggled on, keeping the bows of the *Venus* turned sideways across the cut into the wind.

It was in emerging from a lock that the chief danger lay, for the *Venus* then had had no time to get up a speed, and with speed a resistance: with a weigh on, the propeller blades dug themselves deeper down, rooting the boat more firmly in the water. In addition, at the mouth of each lock the mud and stones were more plentiful than anywhere else, and conspired with the evil wind to catch us prisoner.

It was one continuous battle. The shafts were in our hands almost as constantly as if they were swords and we were fighting for our lives, and if we tired the enemy was tireless. Strands of loose hair whipped into our eyes. Our voices were hoarse from shouting to one another words which were swept out of hearing on the currents of air. Nor did we dare to slacken speed in bridge-holes, but went tearing through at a forbidden rate, sloshing water over the tow-path and sucking mud in our wake to silt up the narrow straits for future unfortunates. We learnt to curse the sight of a horse-boat in the distance, because in passing that we had to slow down and the result was unvaried: the helpless sideways drift, shafts out, hollering, shoving, the engine hammering, the wind triumphant.

Then Cleopatra took it into her senseless little head to go exploring. We all saw her step off and stretch her paws along a beam and sneeze noiselessly and shake her head and yawn. None of us saw her jump aboard again. Her absence was remarked some way farther on when for once we seemed to be holding our own with the gale and getting along fairly smartly.

'Where's Cleopatra?' shouted Charity, first to one of us then the other.

Head shakings in answer. She looked in both the cabins, into the holds, then tucking a bicycle under her arm, prepared to jump off at the next bridge-hole.

'You surely aren't going back for her?' said Nanette.

'Going back for her? – but of course I am. How can we leave her there?'

And astonished at such a heartless suggestion, she nearly missed the bridge-hole, nearly lost her footing, jumped clumsily and landed in a muddle with the pedals spinning round and one trouser-leg torn. However, on finding Cleopatra some half-mile back, tasting grass and lightly waving her tail with no understanding of how nearly she had been abandoned, Charity slapped her soundly and, still scolding, set her on her shoulder. Cleopatra, her yellow eyes crossed with stupefaction and meowing under her breath, at once drove her claws hard into Charity's back. There she stayed, slipping and scrabbling in a perfect fit of terror, her long nails making the return journey one of much pain for Charity, more especially as the front wheel was flat. She overhauled the boats at a bridge-hole and leaping off just managed to fling herself on to the gunwale of the motor-boat as it passed, dragging the bicycle after her by the handle-bars. Quite gently, she disentangled the kitten from her jersey and dropped her into the hold. Emma was steering the *Venus*.

'I don't know what Amos has done to our bicycle,' said Charity, 'but he's done it thoroughly. I was riding on the rims most of the way. There isn't a breath of air in that front tyre. We'll have to use the other bicycle until we get this one mended. So like a little boy.'

Roaming was a new idea with Cleopatra. She who had shown little imagination before, or curiosity, content to sit on the cabin-top licking herself and staring, now became a nuisance. At every lock she had to be our last thought before leaving it. Our last gesture was to snatch her off the side and toss her aboard, and if it was Emma or Nanette who threw her on she usually had a shaking in addition, which taught her nothing, except perhaps to hate us.

The locks, as Charity had said, were not dirty here but they were still the width of a single boat only and the butty still had to be dragged behind by hand. The *Ariadne*, who in front of the wind behaved with no more weight than a dry leaf, seemed at the end of a cotton-line a very different matter, and grew no lighter as the morning went on. Each of us in turn rubbed raw our bare and frozen hands and wore a groove in first one shoulder and then the other. Occasionally the cotton-line fell by accident into the cold water, making it no pleasanter to handle, its thin hard coils having, when wet, the bite of an adder. And again and again the butty, like a cow refusing to be driven to market, ran sulkily on to the mud, and we called her wrathful human names as we pulled and pushed. The wind was so strong we could almost use it as an arm-chair. Such a wind seemed natural to the bleak and foreign country round us: the rare trees were hard-bitten and short-branched, all leaning over in one direction from custom; the rarer cottages held themselves as close to the ground as possible. We passed acres of ploughed land, the deserted ranks of earth inclining one to think that not man but the wind itself had, with its long sweeping gestures, raked them there.

We saw no sign of our own type of craft, though horse-boats we met in plenty and once or twice a horse-boat over-took us. On one occasion we were stranded at the mouth of a lock and bearing it with patience since it was not by any means the first time, and we guessed was not going to be the last, when a horse-boat came into the lock behind us. A young girl, very pretty with a red pouting mouth, came down the path to us and said:

'You on the mud? We'll give you a snatch if you like.'

We thanked her, and she stayed to talk. She wore a bright clean handkerchief tied round her head and under her chin and was plainly yearning for the company of girls. In about three minutes she managed to tell us, either by direct state-ment or inference, that she and her mum and dad all lived in their boat, that she was sick of the life and ashamed to tell young men her home was a boat, that it wasn't right for a girl, that she liked dancing (did we?) and had met an American in a pub the night before, that she was sixteen and her name was Freda, and that their horse was a new one only just bought by her dad and going so fast they hardly knew how to keep up with it.

Still telling us of the horse, she stepped aboard her boat, which by now was coming out of the lock, at the same time off-handedly but with great skill catching the loop of a rope round the stud on the *Venus's* fore-deck and thereby success-fully snatching us off our bank of mud. Her parents seemed to be cheerful people who nodded and smiled at us, looking proudly at Freda and at their horse, which was rushing forward along the tow-path at such a pace that although, thanks to their help, we followed them at top speed, they were soon no more than two specks in the distance.

It was our last lock for some time, and in the succeeding long pound Charity washed a great many underclothes and hung them on a string in the *Ariadne's* hold to dry. She also washed some smalls belonging to Emma and Nanette.

'Not,' she said, 'that I'm washing them clean – it would be silly to try, but I'm freshening them up a bit.'

Even this was dubious as she rinsed them in cold water scooped from the cut, hardly a purifying influence, but certainly they turned a shade lighter and gave us the impression that we were not, in spite of hardship, allowing ourselves to become absolute sluts. Our shirts and jersies we were sensible enough to leave alone, arguing that it was a waste of time to wash away dirt that would replace itself in less than twenty-four hours, and that, in any case, they did not touch our skins. Our blankets were all dark-blue army ones, and so we were able to pass over their condition until such time as they began to smell, when they were sent to the laundry.

Emma was steering the motor, saying that as she had the sharpest temper it was best that she should be to blame if we happened to stick on the mud again. Crab-wise the *Venus* covered the miles. We began to feel happier and to think we were seasoned to the gale and smart enough to fool it. The washing cracked and flapped like canvas on a sailing ship. Smoke twirled up from the two chimneys. We heartened ourselves with cocoa. Charity scrubbed the hatches. Nanette tightened the side-strings and reported that one of the bow-fenders was nearly adrift. Our ears alternately tingled or glowed or ached, and the land about us changed.

Signs of coal appeared. Mountainous slag-heaps half grassed over with a tip at the top. Single-track railways running parallel to the cut and bearing caravans of coal-trucks. More houses. More people on the tow-path chiefly riding bicycles. Bridges became more frequent, and presently the ground began to rise and we reached two uphill locks.

141

Emma said: 'It's our lucky day after all. Twice I thought we were on the mud, and each time we somehow weren't.'

We toiled uphill, with a hollow feeling inside our chests from prolonged buffeting, and the butty like a mill-stone. Somewhere or other the fender fell off, tearing the staples out with it. We only noticed its loss when the butty ran against a lock gate with a vicious jab instead of the usual soft thump.

'We'll have to be careful,' said Charity. 'We can make holes in things with the bows like that, and the lock-keepers will kill us if we bash their gates about.' One of them nearly did. He burst out of his house with unfriendly violence.

'Where's the fender of that there boat?'

'Just dropped off; we've lost it.' Our legs were like cotton-wool; we were too exhausted to be conciliatory.

'Ain't you got a spare one?'

'Yes we have. But there's no time now. Look, boats coming. We'll put it on this evening. We'll be very careful.'

The gates floated open. We shouldered the cotton-line, bent our heads, put our feet one in front of the other: tramp, tramp. Here were gardens beside us and twining fences. We plodded on. Here was a stile and a path worn away from it across a field. We passed it evenly, counting our steps. And so with weariness brought the *Venus* and *Ariadne* to the top and hitched them together again, and set off through scarred and more populous country towards the last flight of locks before Coventry. But not before we had remarked that the boats behind were rapidly overhauling us, and had seen Amos posed heroically on the bows of the leading one.

They caught us within a mile, and we had not enough spirit left to resent their passing. The high wooden cratches which roof over the for'ard part of the holds and rear themselves immediately behind the fore-decks, had been purposely flattened. Mrs. Hutchins, who was made our friend by the patronage of her son, leaned her tall bony figure out from the butty as it swept by. She was handsome in the old style, with ear-rings, and a waist you could span with your hands strapped in by a man's wide leather belt, and with a full black-stuff skirt down to her ankles. Her bare arms were as strong as her husband's; her head was padded with an intricate number of plaits. Beside her in the hatches were two of Amos's sisters, beautiful little girls, wild-haired, with black fierce eyes slanting up towards their ears and the lips of angels. Somewhere out of sight was a baby. Mrs. Hutchins cried out to us:

'Ain't you goin' to take the cratches down? There's the bridge a-comin' this pound.'

Seeing we understood her, she raised her hand with grim friendliness and disappeared into the cabin. She meant by her warning one particular bridge, which we had indeed forgotten, built so low that unless the cratches were taken down our empty boats rode too high in the water to pass underneath it. Nanette and Charity flew up to the bows of the *Venus* and began to undo the strings and tear away the supports that held the cratch in place, Nanette in the hold and Charity standing above her on the fore-deck. The afternoon was nearly half done.

Emma, steering the *Venus*, was reckoning up miles and locks in her head, and balancing them against the hours of daylight and remaining strength. The *Venus* was approaching a bridge-hole. The thought occurred to Emma in the middle of her calculations and just before the bows reached it, that Charity, working with her back towards the bridge, might not have seen it. With a flash of alarm she yelled:

'Charity – look out.'

Charity, instead of ducking her head, inquiringly lifted it. The *Venus* was travelling at five knots and the bridge was stationary, but Charity's neck was not broken. She was flung forward with a groan across the subsiding cratch, which, crumbling under her weight, enveloped Nanette in a jumble of tarpaulin, strings, struts of wood, and Charity. Emma, believing Charity was dead, left the tiller and hurried round the gunwale, but Charity rose up from the wreck of the cratch and came running down the planks to meet her, holding the back of her head with one hand and laughing. Nanette, not knowing what had happened, was crossly trying to beat herself free from folds of tarpaulin.

'You're concussed,' cried Emma, catching hold of Charity's arms so that we both nearly lost our balance. 'You're hysterical, come and lie down. I thought you were dead.'

'Dead?' said Charity. 'No, I'm quite all right, leave me alone. But what a crack. What a surprise.' When she took her hand away it was bloodied. She explained to Nanette the reason for her smothering.

'Fancy being biffed on the head by a bridge,' said Nanette in astonishment. 'I mean, what a big thing not to notice coming at you.'

'I had my back to it, how could I have seen? Bridges don't make any noise.'

'There's blood on your hand; you're bleeding.'

'Well, of course I am, I was hit. But it doesn't hurt. No, Emma,' she burst out impatiently, 'leave me alone, I keep telling you I'm all right. I don't want to lie down, I should hate to. But just look at the boats. Oh, why did you leave them?'

The *Venus* had blundered her own way under the bridge, and made blindly for the nearest grassy bank, by which she was halted. Luckily her bows, not her stern, were on mud; the butty was still knocking about under the bridge. It was a simple matter to reverse the engine and float her off backwards.

'I don't believe,' said Nanette, 'I could lift another shaft today, so you'd better keep clear of mud or get yourself off it. Charity, don't you think that tea would do you good? I've got a dry mouth and a cold stomach. I'm tired of to-day, I wish it was over. I wish I'd been hit on the head, only harder, enough to make me unconscious.'

Charity made the tea. The boats drove on. Our eyelids by this time were as swollen and red as though we had been

144

weeping for days on end, and squeezed tightly together into slits against the villainy of the wind. Our lips had a desert dryness, the muscles of our faces ached. Wind was still everywhere about us, savagely playful, kicking up the water, swooping across the budding branches in gusts of violence that nearly took their summer from them, bullying the *Venus* and *Ariadne*, and even catching up a garment from Charity's line and whirling it out of reach in the giddy air. Seeing this, Charity, who was just appearing out of the butty cabin with mugs of tea, burst into tears and began to climb shakily on to the roof as though she intended to leap ashore and chase it.

'Stop,' cried Nanette, clawing her ankles. 'It wasn't anything of yours. It was a pair of my pants. Leave them, let them go. They wanted mending, I never liked them.'

Charity, with the disconcerting calmness she always showed when weeping, blew her nose and said: 'Then it's a pity I bothered to wash them.'

'I think you've been unstrung,' said Nanette. 'You'd better drink your tea and sit down. What does it matter if something blows away?'

Emma, anxious about the daylight and the state of her crew, called out to a boy pedalling along the path: 'How many miles to the locks?'

He waved his arm backwards over his shoulder and, misunderstanding her question, gave her the idiot answer: 'Straight on.'

'Thank you very much,' she shouted, but her irony was drowned in the wind and the boy went on.

We passed close beside the offices and wash-houses of a coalmine and saw black-faced men walking about with lamps fixed to the centre of their helmets. None of them looked at us or turned their heads as the boats went by. Coal was everywhere, the dust of it blotching the surface of the water, coating the grasses. Here it was still part of the earth, the earth and it stamped indistinguishably together, and it was difficult to say whether the men who tried to divide the two were themselves walking pieces of coal or part of the dark earth. On the other side of the cut long-tailed ponies struggled uphill over the slag, dragging buckets. The air, glittering with coal-dust, was laced with overhead cables. We passed underneath them, and sped on.

How wonderful, thought Emma, that we can pass, anything, everything, all the time. And for a moment exuberance came into her mouth like a taste, and her tiredness lightened. Everything, she thought, we leave behind; nothing can grab hold of us; wretchedness may degrade and hold prisoner others, but not us – we spin by like a humming top and are free. Something of this she tried to say to Charity, who brought her up a mug of tea.

'Yes,' said Charity, her grave brows attentive. 'I know what you mean, I've thought of it myself, especially lately, and I'm not sure it is such a good thing. It may be awfully bad for our characters you know. We escape all the time. It's one long flight; it may get a habit.'

'Charity – how odd you are – to take it so seriously. I didn't mean that at all. It was just an idea.'

'Yes, but such an obvious one. And far more important than you think.'

'Charity,' said Emma in real alarm. 'You're talking nonsense.'

'I've got a headache,' said Charity, looking suddenly rather ill. 'It won't be long now. Look, there's the first lock.'

At the bottom of the locks we found Freda's boat tied up, and Freda and her family leaning in their hatches, the very picture of dejection.

'What's the matter?' we cried. 'Is anything wrong?'

Freda's father gloomily spat. ' 'Orse won't go,' he said.

'Won't *go*? Why ever not?'

'Don't ask me, my girl. I don't know what goes on in an 'orse's 'ead, especially when it's a noo 'orse. I tried 'im all

146

ways, tried 'im with shovin', tried 'im with 'itting, tried 'im with fodder. And what does 'e do? Turns round and starts goin back the way 'e come.' The horse was very peacefully eating the grass beside the tow-path. 'And 'e's stronger nor me,' said Freda's father. 'If 'e says no to budging, no it is. Maybe 'e'll feel different in the morning. 'Orses is funny.'

Freda climbed out past her father with a windlass and said she would lock-wheel for us. We were more thankful to her than we could say. That last flight was almost beyond our strength. It was getting dark by the time we reached the top, and there, with our last ounce of energy, we tied up the boats.

'I think,' said Nanette, 'we ought to leave the engine running for a bit, and the pump on. The engine-room bilges are almost full again. I'm sure they shouldn't fill so fast. I wonder if there's something wrong.'

'I don't know,' said Emma. 'I wouldn't be surprised if the boats fell to bits. At the moment I wouldn't even care. How's your hand?'

'It's hurting,' said Nanette.

Charity called from the butty: 'Could one of you find some coal, the coal-box is empty?'

Coal in those parts was considered common property. It was without any sense of stealing that Nanette filled a bucket two or three times from a coal-boat moored nearby, and replenished the coal-box. There was no one to ask for permission or we would have asked him, and had we asked him he would have helped us fill our bucket. Often, passing a coal-boat, or, in the London district, a coal-barge, the man aboard would toss lumps of coal into our holds as a kindness, or shovel out a heap on the lock-side for us to gather up.

The canal outside the top lock was cluttered with coal-boats, deserted now that the day's work was over, for though Freda and her family lived aboard their boat, most of these local boaters had homes ashore. It was a bad tie-up altogether for there was no water-tap, and both our cans were empty.

'A drink would do us all good,' said Nanette, 'and perhaps they'll give us water in the pub too.'

So to the pub, standing a few yards away, we all went, taking the water-cans and Freda with us. The public bar was already crowded and the longer we stayed the more people came pushing into it. We managed to squeeze up in a corner by the fire, and having once sat down wondered what power was ever going to raise us again. A woman in horn-rimmed spectacles and a cigarette in her mouth was banging away at the piano with fingers of iron, her elbows going up and down. Two soldiers leaned round her asking her to play *Yours*, and *Always* and other tunes of sacred memory. Still banging, she screwed up her eyes and shook her head and they loudly coaxed her to yield. Soon they would begin to sing. Later the whole room would sing, linking arms, sisterly, brotherly, conversation failing, faces in a glow, the night cold outside and somewhere the war still being fought.

But first of all there was the talking to be done. To-day and the days to come were being discussed by separate groups of young fellows and their elders. Beer, that cold amber drink so good for friendship, was being splashed to and fro across the counter. Injustices were being mellowed, conversations repeated more and more untruthfully; man, on every hand, was being turned into superman and the transition went unnoticed.

There was an atmosphere of clean clothes and hands washed under a running tap and to-morrow being the day for a shave, of making the most of to-night and feeling the better for it. In the background was the twinkle of mirrors; darts flashed dangerously between the shifting heads; streams of cigarette smoke closed together, hung, drifted, thickened; and behind the noise, the voices, the terrible piano, to an attentive or a drowsy ear, the fire kept up its small prattle no louder than pins dropping or insects walking through hay. Freda, her social instinct so thoroughly excited, gabbled on and on – about her boys, her haughty words, what her father had said, what her mother had answered. Silent beside her we sat, Emma and Charity, legs stretched out, nodding, burning, hearing every word she said fall bright and clear to float in our stupid wind-exhausted minds like the scraps of coloured cloth in a patch-work quilt, without sense, but warming, soothing.

Nanette wriggled her way back from the bar with half-pint mugs in her hand and by her side a short tough little man wearing a check cap and a tie.

'Hullo Joey,' said Freda.

'How's yourself,' said Joey. He too, it seemed, was a boat-man.

'God bless them,' whispered Nanette, falling into place between Charity and Emma and laying her head on Charity's shoulder. 'Hear how they talk. It's more than I can do. My tongue's paralyzed. I can't say a word. To think to-day's really over – it's too good to be true.'

The soldiers were singing with solemn happiness. Loudly above the din their voices rose, with the commanding slowness of a funeral march and the volume of a bull's bellow. Joey bent his head down to Freda's. She had been telling him of their trouble with the new horse.

'You want to blindfold him,' said Joey, shouting confidentially in Freda's ear. 'That'll soon put him right, you see. You tell your dad to wrap his eyes up and he'll go as quiet as a lamb. I know,' he said, staring from one of us to the other with a challenging air. 'I've had to deal with 'orses all me life. Couple of year back I bought a new 'orse, just like your dad and after I'd paid the money over I found out he was a race-'orse. It's the truth, he was a ruddy race-'orse. Every morning he started out to win the Derby. Well, with a boat tied on, it was awkward. I had to train him. Every time he started off a-galloping, I threw him into the cut. Just so often as ever he tried to be a winner, in he went. He learnt soon enough. Time I'd finished he was a model 'orse, none better.'

Nanette stared unbelievingly at his dwarfish figure and tried to imagine him wrestling with a race-horse. Bands of dizzy golden light and noise pressed down on us. Feeling and sound became the same, the tingling in our feet was one with the words curried thickly about us. Soldiers and pianist had embarked cheerfully on the stamping roaring pleasures of *It's My Brother Sylvest. . .* The press of people turned in a surge towards the piano, mugs in their hands, their mouths bursting joyously open, argument forgotten.

'Time to go,' murmured Emma. 'There's supper to cook. We must wash our faces and get undressed. We must go to bed.'

'Charity,' said Nanette, pushing her flushed face and sleepy eyes close under Charity's nose. 'You look a bit peaky. You haven't said a word. Are you all right?'

'My head's aching,' said Charity. 'Let's go, let's really go.'

She got up and began to thrust her way out through the smoke and crush, with hammers crashing the back of her eyes into splinters and a feeling of sickness in her throat.

'Nanette,' said Emma, befuddled. 'The water – I forgot.' She pulled the empty cans out from under the bench. 'Don't bother – I'll ask the landlord for water, he'll give us some, he must have a tap somewhere. You go on, go after Charity; I don't think she's well.'

12

Long before the alarm clock trilled out its early morning blessing, Emma was awakened by the voice of Nanette calling from the motor cabin. It was still dark.

'What do you want?' she shouted. 'What's the matter?'

'Come here – come here a minute.'

Gluey-eyed and grumbling, Emma rolled her feet on to the floor and fumbled her way outside. The drop from the hatches of the butty to the deck of the motor-boat was more pronounced than usual, but she was not sufficiently awake to notice the difference. She pushed her head into Nanette's frowsy cabin. 'What the hell's the matter?' she said.

'I'm sinking,' said Nanette, and chuckled.

Emma reached forward one hand and switched on the light. The water covering the cabin floor was dark and still. On its surface floated a match-box and scraps of paper. A sock which had recently fallen in was just in the act of drowning. Jersies trailed their empty arms in the rising flood and blankets slipped down towards a soaking grave. Nanette, her hair like a gooseberry bush, sat straight up in bed, her lips parted with excitement.

'I'm going down fast,' she said, with awe in her voice, and glee.

Emma stumbled towards the engine-room, shaking off her petrification. 'Charity,' she shouted. 'Wake up – hurry: the *Venus* is sinking.'

One glance was enough to show the futility of trying to start the engine, and with it the pump; only half the fly-wheel was above water. The engine-room was a black sea of floating oil. She rushed back to the butty cabin, pushed her arms and head into a jersey and threw on an overcoat.

'I'm going to fetch the N.F.S.,' she said to Charity. 'You and Nanette must use the hand-pump – and pump like mad, or it's good-bye to the *Venus*; she's going down like a stone.'

Charity, silent, was already in Wellingtons, tying her dressing-gown round her. Emma snatched the bicycle ashore, flung herself heavily on to it and pedalled off across the bridge. Her bent head and shoulders showed for a moment blackly against a sky that was beginning to be streaked low down with the silver fire and bird-grey tones of morning, and then she was gone.

Together, the one chattering, the other wordless, Nanette and Charity hauled the hand-pump up from the hold and dumped it with a splash into the engine-hole. This clumsy metal drain-pipe was awkward in every way. It slipped to and fro on the steel floor-boards; its spout, leaning outside, rolled round and round, pointing all directions but the right one. It had also secreted somewhere inside it lumps of coal, and every now and again sucked one of these up, choked, and came to a spluttering standstill. As often as this happened the whole monstrous pump had to be lifted out, turned upside down, shaken, and afterwards primed again with a bucketful of water. They laboured at it doggedly, one of them standing inside the engine-hole with water half-way up her shins, holding it steady, the other balanced on the gunwale outside, working her arms up and down as the old men at Limehouse did: up, one; down, two; up, three; losing count, hair in her eyes, sobs on her breath, the night all round her mysteriously and swiftly turning into day and the sky above her rearing up its high and flaming arches. Fifty strokes each, and they changed places. Or they lost the score, and – 'You've done

152

enough,' cried the one inside, noting the flagging arms, the weakening jet of water, and so they changed. Emma was a long time away. The morning was there, the trees were alive, the canal was shining, before she was back with an N.F.S. waggon and a bunch of boisterous men.

A floor-board was prised up in the cabin, the huge nozzle inserted and in only a few minutes the gallons of water were drained away from the inside of the *Venus*, where they had no business to be, and returned to their proper place in the canal. The engine was started and the pump knocked on to keep her from filling again. Tea and cigarettes rewarded everyone, and still in pyjamas and dressing-gowns we stood round and discussed the event with our rescuers.

'There must be a hole in the bottom,' said Nanette, as though we were on the trail of a treasure-trove and had come by accident on the place marked X.

Emma said: 'I dare say we went aground once too often yesterday on something harder than mud.'

'Nah,' said one of the men, chewing his cigarette up like a meal, 'you couldn't spike a hole in her if you tried. She's steel ain't she, not wood?' He kicked the *Venus* and nodded. 'More likely she's got a bolt come loose and dropped off.' He wiped his mouth and slammed his mug down on the cabin-top, grateful to us as we were grateful to him. 'Go slow,' said he. 'Keep the pump a-going and you'll be all right I reckon. She ain't leaking faster than that there pump can empty.'

They were not in the least sullen at being roused so early. Into their truck with cheerful grins they piled. 'You're welcome,' they answered when we shouted out our final thanks.

'Takes a man . . .' said one young hulk, waving. The hour was fresh and fragrant without wind, of virgin purity, unquickened by the sun, a world of light without shadow, of shapes without colour. Off, in a burst of speed, went those three stout men. As soon as they were gone we began to discuss more quietly what next we ought to do.

153

'Either,' said Emma, 'we can phone forward to Coventry and get a repair-gang out here, or we can hope the leak doesn't grow any worse and carry on till we get there. We'll keep the pump going, and if it gets worse we'll have to bale as well.'

'I don't see that a repair gang could do anything to us here,' said Nanette. 'She'll have to go into dry-dock before they can find out where the hole is.'

'What do you think, Charity?'

Charity had been markedly silent. Now she said: 'I think I shall have to go home. There's something wrong with my head. I couldn't sleep last night and my eyes are hurting.'

We looked at her in consternation, the *Venus* forgotten.

'Charity . . . why didn't you *say*?'

'I was waiting to see if it got worse and it has. I think I shall have to go home. I think,' she said, 'it might be serious.'

'You've probably cracked your skull,' said Nanette. 'How awful for you. I knew of a man who cracked his, and he had to have it riveted together with bits of silver. It doesn't show, but I think it stops your hair from growing.'

'Charity, are you well enough to travel?'

'Oh dear, yes, of course. I'm not ill. It's just my head that hurts, and my eyes too.' She went softly into the cabin and began to pack her things. We looked at one another, feeling the cold air pinching our ankles for the first time.

'What a morning,' said Nanette. 'It isn't eight o'clock yet and already the *Venus* has nearly sunk and Charity's cracked her skull. Of course she really did that yesterday, but we didn't know then.' Leaning forward she whispered: 'That man, the one who cracked his skull – he died. First he went mad, then he died.'

'I don't believe you,' cried Emma in horror. 'You're making it up. How can you.'

'It's quite true,' said Nanette with a ghastly expression. 'I never knew him myself. He was a friend of my aunt's, the one in the Foreign Office; she never tells lies. A spar fell on his head in a storm. Don't tell Charity.'

154

Gloomily we ate our last breakfast together. Charity had the pallor of death already in her face and rings of tiredness round her eyes. Wondering if we should remember in a year's time the sound of her voice, we listened with unhappy attention to the few words she spoke, and pathetic indeed was the sight of her thin bony fingers unhurriedly picking up and laying down her slice of bread and marmalade: so soon they might be crossed on her breast and her breast weighted with earth. We glanced at her sideways sentimentally, suffering a positive indigestion from the pressure of a newly discovered affection. As for Charity, she ate stoically, and any thoughts of death she kept to herself.

'Shall I take Cleopatra with me?' she said once, stroking the cat's tail.

'No. Of course not. Leave her with us.'

'But will you look after her? Will you remember to feed her?'

We swore we would.

'Don't let her lose herself. You will go back for her, won't you, if she gets left behind?'

We promised to care for Cleopatra more than we cared for ourselves.

We saw her to the station, walking at the speed of a funeral cortege. We carried her bag for her, we bought her ticket for her, we found her an empty carriage, we settled her in a corner seat. Charity bore it all patiently. She might have been searching in her mind for the last line of a sonnet, so quiet and abstracted was she. Just as the train moved she sprang up and leaned actively out of the window, fixing on first one of us and then the other a glance of warm sincerity. 'See you soon,' she cried out, suddenly excited and impatient. She looked back at us as the train drew away and appeared to be laughing. Waving wretchedly, smiling horribly, we saw her disappear, a dying beauty, and our hearts were like lead. It seemed so sad.

'I wonder if one of us ought to have gone with her,' said Nanette. 'She was awfully strange.'

It was too late to think of that. She was gone. We tramped sorrily back to the boats and considered sinking the *Venus* deliberately as a colossal sacrifice, or going back to bed, for the joy had been taken out of the day, and the spring of our youth, we were certain, was blighted for ever.

'Of course,' said Nanette, 'she may get better. She's young after all, and very resilient. That man who died was older. He was a friend of my aunt's so he must have been fifty at least, and at that age people die easily anyway.'

So we smothered our grief and plucked up our spirits and set the leaky *Venus* limping forward to Coventry with the pump spouting away and bursts of sunlight passing over like flocks of birds wheeling across the country sky.

We arrived at the work-shop with its adjoining dry-dock at about ten-thirty and explained our predicament and had our leakage diagnosed. It had a more serious cause than a missing bolt. We needed, said the man, after walking about for some time underneath the boat and taking up the floor-boards in the cabin, a new stern-bush – the metal box and packing which enclosed the propeller shaft. He was very slow and grave in his summing-up and added that it was Saturday. We begged him to hurry, having no wish to stay boxed up in a dry-dock over the week-end. Still shaking his head he set to work, and after watching him for some time we retired to the *Ariadne* which was tied up outside the dry-dock, for it seemed incongruous to sit inside a boat anchored in air.

Over the inevitable mug of cocoa we talked of Charity and our immediate future. A third hand to replace the loss of Charity was desirable, but difficult to find. We delved amongst our friends and relations, turning out and discussing every possibility and several frank impossibilities. It amounted to this: everyone we knew was either engaged in some form of warfare, or too old and feeble to turn a windlass.

'We'll have to go two-handed,' said Emma. 'It'll be slower and more difficult, and much more tiring, and we may even kill ourselves, but it is possible. It is done, after all.'

'It's done by boys,' said Nanette stubbornly, 'but it's all wrong for girls to do it. It's too hard for us.'

'Well, I agree with you. I hate the idea myself, especially with you – it would almost be like going one-handed. But just suggest someone else.'

'Wilfred,' said Nanette, mentioning a new name and plainly delighted by her thought. She went on to say that Wilfred was in the Navy and at the moment on sick-leave. 'He's just who we want,' she said. 'A man is so much better than a girl because of being strong, and as he's in the Navy we shan't have to explain about ropes, and port and starboard, and things like that. He's a Commander,' she added, vaguely screwing up her eyes, 'or a Captain, I'm not sure which. I'll write to him straight away.' And this, without further hesitation, she did.

It never occurred to us that an invitation to visit our boats could be other than a perfect treat for whoever it was to whom we tendered it. A request to join our crew must be proportionately more flattering. There were many, we thought in genuine innocence, who would give their ears for such a chance, and few who were lucky or free enough to profit by it. So the letter was sent off to Wilfred under the pleasant impression that we were offering him the time of his life.

This done, we searched out the spare fender and carried it up to the bows of the *Venus*, together with a box of staples, a length of tarred string, a hammer and the bread-knife. Squatting down we began the task of fixing it over the naked steel ridge which otherwise could cause such damage. Or more exactly, Emma fastened the fender on and Nanette crouched by nursing her right hand, for the gash she had torn on a rusty nail refused to mend and was troubling her. Considering it was always dirty, smeared with oil, bumped and licked and bleeding all day long, the wonder is it ever healed and left her no more than a purple mark as reminder. The Bottom Road had scarred her. In time it scarred us all. Nanette said suddenly:

'Will Charity die, do you think?'

'I don't know,' answered Emma indifferently, for in those under-twenty days of mad egotheism affection for another person required the actual presence to keep it alive, and concern perished quickly without the wind of drama to fan its flame. A staple was sinking crookedly into the wood and she occupied herself in straightening this for a few moments. Then she said. 'She'll probably live to be very old. There's something awfully tough about Charity, although she always looks so white and sickish.'

'I hope she falls in love and marries young,' said Nanette. 'I do think as a spinster she'd be frightening.'

Emma went on banging away for a bit, thinking of Charity. Then she took a staple out of her mouth and remarked: 'The trouble with her is she doesn't reason. She's full of convictions instead. That's why you can't argue with her.'

'I've never tried,' said Nanette.

'Well, I wouldn't if I were you. She'd make a wonderful Bloody Mary, burning people left and right for the sake of her conscience, or justice or duty or something, and crying all the time. It wouldn't be any use appealing to her either; she's inflexible. Yes, she's inflexible.'

'Crying all the time,' echoed Nanette. 'That's what's so funny about her. She cries *prodigiously*. I'd be ashamed, but Charity isn't.'

'It's probably something to do with her upbringing. Her father was a bishop, you know.'

'No, I didn't know,' said Nanette.

'He was a bishop and then he died, and her mother married again, some kind of chemist I think. Anyway he's terribly clever and Charity adores him. He's the one who's always sending her telegrams.'

'I wonder what her mother's like,' said Nanette, with a note of fruity preface in her voice.

'That's enough,' cried Emma hastily, giving the staple a last bang and gathering up tools and oddments as she rose. 'Don't start on *your* mother. No, no – don't say another word. I don't want to hear.' And she fled away, dropping the string as she ran and scattering staples into the hold.

'You're very rude,' shouted Nanette. Instead of following she stayed where she was, astride the new fender, idly kicking her legs and speculating on a good many agreeable mysteries, including herself.

By one o'clock the *Venus* had been equipped with a new stern bush and we were spared the indignity of a Sunday in dry-dock. No loading was done on a Saturday afternoon or Sunday and the office where, on Monday morning, we should take our orders, was only a couple of miles away. There was nothing to do for thirty-six hours.

'I can't bear the thought of cooking a meal,' said Emma, who never could bear this particular thought. 'Let's tie up the boats and go and get something to eat in a cafe.' We had learnt to pronounce this word as an English one, without its accent.

We stopped the boats at the next bridge, tied them up to rings, smeared lipstick over our dirty mouths, stuffed some money in our pockets, padlocked the cabins, and ran up the long road with its avenue of slag-heaps in search of dinner. We were given meat pie and sloppy cabbage in the first cafe we came to, and found ourselves at the end of it with a free afternoon in front of us and a feeling of dissatisfaction worse than boredom.

'When I'm cross,' said Nanette, looking thoroughly so, 'I always feel too fat. It's most disagreeable because I'm not fat, I'm just plump, and plump women are meant to be attractive, aren't they, so I ought to be glad.'

'Nonsense,' said Emma. 'You're downright fat, and it isn't attractive, it's disgusting. Everybody thinks so.'

'Then,' said Nanette, flushing, 'how do you account for. . . .'

'Oh, I know – all your beastly men. I can't think. They must be mad.'

Nanette said candidly: 'I don't really know a lot, I wish I did. And I don't know any very well.'

So the little show of bad-temper fizzled and went out, for the idea of a Saturday afternoon in Coventry was the real root of our discontent and we both of us knew it. The cafe where we sat belonged to an outlying district which had once been a separate village and would never be village again. Our elbows were planted amongst the dirty china. It was after two o'clock.

'Let's take a bus right into Coventry and see a Saturday afternoon at its most horrible,' said Emma.

'I don't want to,' said Nanette.

'We ought to. We mustn't avoid it. We live in other places and pretend it doesn't happen, but it does, every week of lots of people's lives.' She was remembering Charity's words the previous day and trying to turn them into sense. Nanette said:

'Saturday afternoon in a big town – it's *beastly*. It's shiny and gross and discreet. It's like touching satin with rough hands. I'd rather shut my eyes. I'd rather live somewhere else. I'd rather be comfortable. Let them get on with their Saturday afternoon, anyone who wants to. I'd rather go to sleep till it's all over.'

'No, no,' cried Emma, hauling her out of her seat. 'Don't be so smug, it's cruel. Anyone in Coventry might have been us. We're only lucky.'

'You sound like Charity,' said Nanette, complaining. 'Only it comes worse from you.'

We paid for our food and got on the next bus that passed.

We found Coventry at its most raw and failed to be as mortified by it as Emma had thought good for us. The pavements were crowded, the shops were full of garish goods, the faces of girls going arm-in-arm and giggling were joyless,

160

ill-painted, even the bombed churches showered down no dignity; but we escaped. Charity would have identified herself distressfully all the time with all she disliked and pitied. The cheap high heels would have clattered directly across her heart. The young men we saw thronging the street-corners on the look-out for no known satisfaction, emotions impoverished, bones undeveloped, spoiled by the century of their country's inheritance, of the dreamy creamy cloudy wisdom, half-earth half-animal, of the countryman, he who lives through a lifetime of seasons and dies young compared with his apple-trees – uprooted young men with their instinct stolen away: their unremarkable punishment would have hung a heavy cross round Charity's neck. But not round our necks.

We lacked the gift of sacrifice; faults not ours we could not share, we could not pity. And so we should always escape the blame of Saturday afternoons such as this one, escape and rejoice, possibly to be crushed later by disaster personal enough to crack the nutty casing of our natural selfishness, acid enough to eat away the soft inward kernel, the small white heart.

But for the moment we were safe. We were wearing boots, we were dirty, we were alien, we were immune. And the day turned into a sort of celebration. With a new buoyancy we raided shop after shop, buying such things as tooth-paste and dish-cloths, and shouldered our way through crowds, and found ourselves round about tea-time in the backwater of a dark little book-shop somewhat exhausted but wearing our happy tempers like haloes.

Book-shops have an international personality, a calming reflective personality, uninfluenced by place or time or fashions, even by wars. That stored and dusty smell, how rich it is. We lingered for nearly an hour, and we might have been anywhere, anywhere in the world. An old man pottered about in the background and although he took no notice of us, we sensed we were welcome. Finally we dragged ourselves away from the shelves' narcosis, Nanette buying a copy of *The Polyglots*, and Emma a dull and ponderous biography of Cromwell which she never opened again. And then at the door we turned back to pay for an edition of *The Wild Flowers of England* with 1875 printed on the fly-leaf. That small mildewed volume with its picture of a dog-rose on the first page and its gentle collection of other weeds, spread a fragrance over the whole eccentric day.

Later in the evening as we waited for a bus, Nanette was seen and pounced on by a friend of hers, a doctor, and this seemed so astonishing to all of us that we thought no more about our boats until nearly eleven o'clock, when the last bus had gone and we were forced to find ourselves stranded in a strange city.

The doctor, whose name was Owen, said he knew some people, Quakers, who lived only a little distance away and would surely give us shelter. He rang them up, and without hesitation they offered us two beds. Afraid of being misjudged by these kind people, we stopped under a street-lamp outside their garden gate and ate a quantity of tooth-paste to take the beer from our breaths. With the unpleasant taste of peppermint in our mouths and the long day tagged untidily behind us, all we wanted was to say a polite good-night and obliterate ourselves in bed. Instead however, blinking and suddenly embarrassed by our rough and clumsy appearance, we found round a bright fire under bright lights a brisk game of Happy Families going on. Besides the old man and his wife, who were entertaining us, was a younger woman, probably a relative, and an ill, proud little boy of twelve, wide awake with a will of steel.

Down we all sat and a new hand was dealt and gravely we plunged into the battle for possession of Mr. Chips and Mr. Soot. And again – again how remote, belonging to another existence, seemed the beginning of the day, that morning when the *Venus* had been sinking. How real was the dislike with which we presently eyed the child Edward as he faced us with his mouth tight and triumphant, and every family under his hand.

At midnight we stood up to drink Horlicks and eat biscuits. Owen went backwards out of the door with a tired grin still fixed across his face, and we never saw him again. The pretty straight-up Edward kicked the fire and refused to go to bed. We chatted. The room swam. We heard the soft inquiring voices distantly. By half past twelve we were both asleep.

13

Sunday was a vacuum, a day that did not move forward, as most days do, from morning, through afternoon, to evening, but was immediately on waking all three together, morning, afternoon and evening, and so remained breathless, an unprogressive lull from first to finish. Nanette, before breakfast, came into Emma's room, her nakedness wrapped in a counterpane, and sat on the end of the bed.

'Can you believe,' she said, 'that a week ago it was snowing – you remember, the Silvers and the mud? It seems like a year since then. Isn't it quiet – is everyone asleep still? My feet were so dirty I slept with my socks on. Emma, what's the time – when do you think we can go?'

How strange it always is to spend an odd night in the house of unknown people whom one will never see again. We looked out of the window on a croquet-lawn and on flower-beds that were another person's recreation. Neatness and wealth were apparent everywhere in a close harmony. We bathed, and felt cleaner but even stranger, drying ourselves with a peculiar coyness with the bath-mat, since we had brought no towels with us and shrank from the dazzling purity of the ones laid out.

After breakfast Nanette played a game of croquet with our host, and Emma inspected the rose-garden and helped to feed the chickens. Edward was spending the day in bed. There were no animals. Polite but impatient, grateful without being really touched, we were by this time anxious to be kings again aboard our own boats. Before lunch, refusing invitations to stay for it, we rushed away headlong, and only later regretted behaving like bears.

In those days we belonged passionately to the country, and towns were no more than passing adventures. We were exact mirrors of the weather, our spirits dashed by a cloud passing and uplifted by the following race of sunlight. Not a bud swelled but we expanded with it, not a straw glistened but our eye possessed it. The noise of the wind meeting branches was voice enough, and the birds were sweet parrots. Opium dreams faint and smoky, were the stories we told one another of our ancestors and of our homes. We were put out by the earth as it puts out young plants to grow and open. Those were the days of a strength carried as lightly as the new leaves blossomed on the old trees, when love was given, not to people, but to curious horizons, and lay stacked within us hot and fuming, like hay. Once in a lifetime, early in life, arises and breaks a wave of pure experience that drenches head and heart and, rinsing away, leaves only in memory a white and glittering sand, untrodden by foot, unvisited again. Such a flood engulfed us now.

We spent the afternoon attending affectionately to the various minor needs of our boats. We spliced on new side-strings where the previous ones had been rubbed or broken away. We painted the chimneys blacker, and redecorated with paint the patches on bows and sterns. Free of obligations, we idled and whistled and bickered, made and drank tea, baled the butty hold dry, overhauled the ropes, and greeted with friendly cries the pair of other empty boats that arrived in the evening and tied up behind us.

The air was balmy. Even the boaters seemed to feel it and instead of falling into the usual excesses of scrubbing and other work, loitered on the tow-path, chatting. They were a newly-married couple, smiling and handsome to look at. Had we heard, they said, of Ernie Foss who had been sacked for refusing to go on the Bottom Road? And they quoted him saying: 'I married me wife to be a wife, not a bloody 'orse.'

Then we told them of our stern-bush and how we had nearly sunk, and realized from them what an excellent story it was with the N.F.S. and Charity's head thrown in.

Then they told us of the motor-tyre picked up on the second flight of locks, and we went over the Bottom Road, agony by agony and story for story, finding it very good stuff on which to build a friendship. And although there is little to say about that Sunday and nothing important happened, it was a very pleasant day, windless and leisurely, when small sounds carried clearly and voices were musical, when the sun shone on for longer than usual and the night was less cold.

14

Monday was a day of coal. Also Spring, yesterday so confident, had taken one step backwards and disguised herself in a drizzle of rain. Emma bicycled along the tow-path to the office, which was still closed, and queued outside the door with Alf, the young husband, and several other boaters whose craft were tied in different parts of the cut. For fifteen minutes we kicked our boots outside and sucked cigarettes and looked dispassionately up at the sky; then the manager arrived by car, wearing a stiff black trilby hat like a doctor's, and opened the little hut to business. Emma was first. She handed her trip-card across the counter and asked for letters. He gave her a packet, together with a telegram for Charity, and asked how things were.

'All right,' said Emma absently, hunting through the various handwritings. She opened the telegram, and after reading it, crumpled it up and threw it on the floor. By this time Charity's stepfather had been able to say more to her than he could in a telegram.

'Had trouble with your stern-bush, I see,' said the manager as he marked her trip-card. Hold-ups, and the reasons for them, were always put down on the card.

'Yes, we did,' said Emma looking up. 'I forgot. We spent Saturday in dry-dock. But it's all right now. Oh, of course – and we've lost our mate. You remember Charity, the dark girl?'

'What happened to her?'

'She was hit on the head by a bridge. We've asked a friend of ours to come and help instead. Is it all right?' She blushed and added: 'It's a man.'

'Well, I don't know,' said he. 'That's your affair I suppose.'

'He's an *old* friend,' she told him. He shrugged his shoulders.

'I'm sorry to hear about your mate,' he said. 'You girls ought to be careful.'

'We are. But you can't help accidents. It's a wonder we don't have more of them.'

'You will,' he answered, grinning. He was a kindly little fellow who had served a good many of his earlier years in the Navy and now had a daughter about the same age as Emma, not on the cut. He told Emma where she was to load and looked after her sighing, a fund of advice in his eyes. He thought of his daughter, and then he thought of girls in general, and they made him sigh again and shake his head.

'Come on in Alf,' he called through the open door. 'How's the missus? D'you want a new mate yet? Wish you was back with the boys I dare say.'

Alf shambled in, too pleased to be able to say a word, silently exposing his still unrotten teeth and glancing back at his friends, the other boaters, who pushed their heads round the door to answer for him. The pale grey drizzle increased. The sky crept down. Into the office floated the sound of a paddle falling, the crack of a whip, a man's voice shouting to his horse.

Nanette, in the meantime, was being entertained by Alf's new missus, Lily. Photographs of the wedding were shown her. She was surprised, but took care to say the right things. A wedding ashore in a church, with Alf in a suit and Lily in a white dress, was something almost impossible to believe. But there they were, before her eyes, as awkward as one could wish, and as extraordinary to see as a couple of their own wild wolfish dogs clipped and beribboned to look like two French poodles. Nanette had thought of canal weddings as something very different, as tribal and splendid and nothing to do with the English Prayer Book. She had vaguely imagined dancing and feasting round a fire, with somewhere a touch of ceremonial blood.

Not a bit of it! There are none who embrace orthodoxy with greater ardour than the canal boaters. Like the graceful savage who puts on Western boots to be progressive, there is pathos in their determination to be respectable. They cannot read – they know it; houses, which make the bargemen their superiors, may be unfamiliar; they may never have travelled in a train, or seen the sea, or spoken through a telephone, but they can at least be married and buried as well as all the people in the unsizeable world they know so little about, but to whose scorn ('gipsies gipsies' shout the children on the tow-path) they are so sensitive. And their morals, they could proudly add, are above reproach, are narrow almost to the exclusion of breathing. If a young man takes a girl to the pictures, he is courting her, and no other girl from that moment may be treated to more than a 'how d'you do' and a nod. If a woman talks to someone else's husband, and the wife not by, she runs the risk of serious calumny.

'You're a scholar, ain't you?' said Lily. She handed Nanette a sheet of paper and watched her face attentively while she was reading. It was a typewritten letter of congratulations and good wishes from the Company. Lily kept it among her wedding photographs.

Presently she asked if Nanette was being courted. Nanette, to oblige her, said that she was, and gave a description of the first man who came into her head as her faithful sweetheart, adding extra touches of darkness and height to please Lily better.

She thought as she talked what a pity it was that in two years time Lily would look ten years older, with her face

171

creased and her voice harsher and the brown bright hair in draggles, for married women with babies alive or coming had no time to spend on their appearances. Mirrors were for the courting girls, and not often referred to again once those brief alluring days were over. The canal women have a short and early blooming. After having exchanged their father's boats for the boats of a husband and carried across their dowry of lace curtains and brass knobs, hard hard work is their portion till they die. The beauty of a woman's face and figure has to be of a very high order to survive such an exercise, and the sorrows that go with it. Often it was only from the lustrous little girls that we could guess how handsome their mothers, still young women, once had been. 'Bronchitus' was the name of every disease that came the way of the boaters, and when the babies died, as they often did – for tinned milk is not the best diet for any but the toughest babies – the sickness that carried them off was bound to be bronchitis. Lily told Nanette of her cousin Vera whose bronchitis had been misunderstood.

'We had to fetch a doctor to her,' said Lily, 'and he said she were prignant. "Oh no she aint," I said, "I know our Vera. She ain't marrit and she don't go with the men. It's bronchitus," I said, and bronchitus it wore. She died on it,' said Lily triumphant, 'ten days after.'

There was Emma, loading order and trip-card between her teeth, Alf decorously bicycling a little distance behind her. The boats were taken astern up a narrow arm of water; close beside it ran the rails on which the coal-trucks came down and unloaded. On the other side was a thorn hedge with blunted trees leaning out from it. No road was in sight, and only one cottage. The grass was saturated with coal-dust; it was piled high between the silver rails; the water was blackened with it. The loading place, narrow at the best of times, was further impeded by two rotting hulks of boats, chained together and half-submerged. As we poled our way backwards a line of trucks was just lumbering down the slope towards us. Two

172

men came out from the shack where they had been warming themselves and drinking tea, and two more rode down with the trucks. Their clothes might have been washed daily in a solution of the coal they spent their lives shovelling; their leather faces were touched by the same dye and had long ago ceased to resemble pink and white flesh. Only their neckerchiefs escaped, being clean for Monday morning. They were cheerful men, though not talkative, and got to work at once.

Boat and truck were laid alongside one another. The flap of the truck was let down, and out in a rattling flood gushed the coal. The first torrent they guided as best they could with the backs of their spades, using them as shields to direct the coal inwards instead of wasting over the edges of the chute on to the path. When the rush had subsided, they took their spades away and climbing into the truck began to shovel out the coal with rhythmic swinging movements.

The *Venus* and *Ariadne* were loaded simultaneously. Emma with a shovel in the hold of one boat, and Nanette with a shovel in the other, scrambled about spreading the coal levelly as it poured in and every now and then drawing the *Venus* or the *Ariadne* a few feet farther along the bank, so that the influx streamed in filling and weighing down first the stern ends then the midships, and then the for'ard part of the holds until the gunwales were only a few inches above the water.

Then we paused and took stock. Tea was made and given to the men. The mugs in their hands and the cigarettes spiked into the middle of their faces were blobs of white as brilliant as snow-drops breaking through the winter ground. They were otherwise black from head to foot, and so were we. Our ears, our necks, our lashes, the insides of our nostrils, were coated with coal-dust. Our throats were gritty with it. Pebbles of coal rolled inside our boots, and although we had taken care to close the hatches, coal-dust had crept in through the cracks and everything we touched in the cabins, every cushion and every kettle, had the same dark deposit.

We suggested, more as a feeble attempt at authority than as a real complaint, for we were quite ignorant, that the *Venus* rode at an angle, tilting over to one side.

'She's all right,' said the head loader. 'She'll settle herself once she gits a-goin'. Coal allus shifts around a bit.' And he added, to silence us, that he had been loading boats for twenty years. 'Git out of it,' he said, waving Alf and his missus forward to their smutty christening. 'We got more'n you to do this mornin'.'

We changed places with the other boats, our own reduced as though by the shame of our dirty condition, theirs still unhumbled, riding high in the air and speckless.

With a cargo of coal it was not necessary, though some did it, to put up the top-planks. We laid them flat along the coal instead, and strapped the side-cloths across them. We did without the top-cloths too, and clothing-up was altogether a simpler and far quicker affair than it had been in London. We tied the last knot, dipped our hands overboard in the cut and started the engine.

The fine rain, which for the last hour had held off, began drifting in across the fields again as we turned the boats into the main canal and headed towards the office from where Emma had earlier fetched the loading orders. The usual racy fast-stepping horses were spanking along the tow-path with boats tied to their shoulders and brasses jingling on their chests.

The day was dismal, not particularly cold, but clammy, and the country, though partly obscured by driving mists, was plainly given over to one purpose: coal. Occasionally we saw distant chimneys, and at one point passed close beneath a group of seven monster funnels whitish in colour with their waists nipped in like horrible females. Coal was everywhere on the move, in large and little quantities, swung aloft in buckets, being shovelled on and off the wharves, loaded here, unloaded there, and the men and horses bent on this occupation were like ants moving sugar, speechless and busy.

The office stood at a point where the canal made an acute hairpin bend. Here also branched off another arm of the cut. Here also was a public-house, a shop, a number of cottages, and a single lock not more than a foot or so deep where the boats were gauged on passing through. It was not therefore a quiet piece of water. Boats, motor or horse-drawn, were always converging on it from one of the three directions, jamming together, fouling each other on the corner, waiting their turn for the lock, or attempting to push through out of turn. It was, to say the least of it, flustering. The manager, who from his office commanded a fine view of this Piccadilly of the cut, had a habit of banging on the window and excitedly beckoning or shaking his head. Another lesser official bounded to and fro with his measuring rod, note-book and pencil, gauging the boats as they lay one by one inside the lock. The shop-bell tinkled, the boaters' wives scrambled to do their shopping, thrusting their heads from the door every few seconds to see if they were being left behind; and the sounds of hooves stamping, engines banging, and that lusty argot of the cut, a mixture of curses, friendly and angry, loaded the air. We approached this hubbub nervously, praying for a lull.

The method of bringing a boat round the hairpin bend was simple: a long cotton-line was tied to the stud on the fore-deck, someone standing on the tow-path wound this line two or three times round one of the bollards ashore and the motor was then put hard ahead; the steerer held the tiller-handle over to the right and the stern swung across while the boat herself, tied by the nose, was unable to move forward. Thus she turned almost on her axis, and, once facing round the bend, the line was unwound and tossed aboard and the boat allowed to go ahead. It was not, with only two of us, so easy to manage, but we left the butty-boat without a steerer and tied her close up to the *Venus* so that she was brought round the corner as a dog brings his tail.

There was a hammering on the window. We looked round distractedly to see the manager waving a telegram at us. 'For Charity,' we thought, but we were wrong: it was from Wilfred. He would come, said the telegram, and would meet us that evening at Braunston. Emma grappled with the problems of gauging. Boats were lining up on the other side of the lock, waiting for her to be done and out of the way. Waiting agreed with no one. She ran to and fro in such a flurry that she muddled herself. Nanette in as great a flurry snatched up water-cans and shopping-bags, leaving the cans under a tap to fill themselves while she hastened away to the shop for food and drink. Reappearing with a weight of tins and bottles and loaves of bread, she cried out:

'Wilfred – where will he sleep?'

Emma was winding a paddle. She shouted back: 'Why, in your cabin of course.'

Nanette rushed off to fetch her water-cans, by this time over-flowing all over the path. We came together again on the end of a rope, lugging the *Ariadne* into the lock. Nanette said, puffing:

'Will that be all *right*?'

'Will what . . . I don't know what you're talking about.'

'Wilfred – in my cabin.'

'Well, don't be silly – you won't be there too.' Then, noticing the shadow of disappointment on her face: 'Nanette, how could you? The boaters would never help us again. You know what they are – they'd hate us. We'd be finished on the cut for ever.'

The boaters were beginning to shout. There was a threatening movement before and behind.

'Nanette, the snubber. . . .' She disappeared into the butty cabin. Nanette began to haul out the soggy yards of snubber coiled under the for'ard deck of the *Ariadne*, drenching her jersey inside with nervous sweat as the mist bedewed its outside.

176

'Emma,' she screamed, her voice muffled by her bent head. 'Where are you?'

With thick wads of bread and cheese in her fist, Emma leapt aboard the *Venus* and pushed the accelerator.

'Must have food,' she said, dropping a slice overboard. 'It's a three-and-a-half-hour pound. Nanette, get *off*.' For Nanette was on the wrong boat and the *Venus* was moving. 'You'll have to sleep in the butty,' she added at the top of her voice, to clinch the interrupted argument. 'He can have your bugs instead of you. Oh, you fool, there's a knot in the snubber.'

'It's not my fault,' yelled Nanette. 'Fool yourself. You ought to have seen it sooner.' The snubber ran out to its full length and the knot tightened past any hope of human undoing, Nanette scrambled aboard the *Ariadne* in a heat of hurry and indignation. A boater had thrust the tiller ready for her into the helm. The man from the office dumped her forgotten water-can on the cabin-top.

'In a proper state, ain't she?' said he, with a grin jerked towards the now distant Emma.

'She's a beast,' said Nanette, meaning it heartily. 'Oh, quick – give me Cleopatra – the kitten, there.'

Horses were on the move, ropes were being unhitched. Cleopatra was hurled after her, and screwing the cat up in one angry hand she suffered herself to be drawn clear of this confusion and carried forward towards three hours of solitude and country.

The mist increased. In the country it was nearly a fog. The air grew colder. Emma dived into the motor cabin and, after rummaging there, came into view again with her own clothing supplemented by pieces of Nanette's wardrobe. Nanette, following her example, hunted through the butty cabin and borrowed from the jumble of clothes belonging to Charity and Emma. Crowned in one another's hats we waved and pirouetted amiably, and feud was forgotten.

It was too wet to read. There was no third hand to relieve either of us of our long vigil. The pound itself presented no problems of steering to engage our attention. We drove on interminably it seemed. In each cabin a fire was burning; each of us kept a kettle boiling, and refreshed ourselves from time to time with a cup of this or a cup of that. Emma found in Nanette's cupboard a secret hoard of biscuits, and the face she turned back towards Nanette was as full of reproach for such duplicity as Nanette's answering glance reproached her for eating them, one by one, until they were finished. However, in the butty cabin were sultanas and other delicacies, and Nanette was able to revenge herself with a thoroughness that presently made her feel sick.

With nothing to do but stand and steer, everything we passed was interesting. The farms we slowly wound around were scrutinized from every angle. Ducks amused us, swimming in our wakes with clamorous beaks. Cows came heavily down to drink and our passing boats sucked away the water from under their noses. We saw their eyes turning with stupid wonder and heard the loud suspicious breaths they blew at the host of fine ripples breaking back against their forelegs. Oh, the slow considerations of the beast, the wily perspicacity of the birds, how much they entertained us. And so did notices in fields and carts in the distance and people on the tow-path, until in a stretch of country more lonely than usual we came upon a sheep caught fast by its wool to a spike of barbed wire. It was struggling intermittently, as though utterly feeble. The ground round it was stamped clear of grass. It must have been there a long time. A hedge partly concealed it and the field behind sloped uphill. No other sheep were in sight, nor was there anyone, boy or man, to whom we could call.

'Poor thing,' yelled Emma, pointing.

The boats drifted by at half-speed. Nanette wondered if the wire was in its flesh or tangled only in the fleece. On a sudden impulse she caught up a kitchen knife and, shouting out to

178

attract Emma's attention, jumped overboard at an opportune bridge-hole and ran back along the path to free the creature.

It was thoroughly frightened and tried to butt her legs as she approached. Never a great success with animals, Nanette was not certain if sheep, when desperate, bit, and circled it cautiously with her knife held in front of her ready for a jab. It rolled its eyes back and stood trembling. She came up in its rear, pounced and took a firm hold on the wool, astonished at the depth and soft masses of it. The sheep, terrified, drummed its hooves on the ground and attempted to rush forward. She found that the barbed wire was intricately wound into the fleece, every attempt to get away having twisted it deeper and tighter. Her knife was useless, the blade slipping bluntly across the wool without cutting it. She gave up the attempt in a few moments and wandered through the mist instead, shouting for help.

Her feet strayed by accident on to a rough path and this she followed uphill, sliding backwards at every step. She was short of breath when she reached the top, but determined by this time to find the sheep a saviour. The mist was lolling about in vapours that sometimes thinned right away to show her a hedge and a great tract of open land beyond it, and sometimes closed in so thickly round her that she was bewildered and fancied herself lost. She left the path and struck off across the hedge, believing she had caught a glimpse of farm buildings. After going a few yards she was lost indeed. The ground sloped down all round her and she had forgotten which way turned her towards the canal.

She retraced her steps through the wet tussocky grass and instead of arriving back at the hedge, found herself amongst a large number of sheep. Fat lambs and well-contented mothers lifted their heads in surprise. She remembered her particular sheep with disgust. Now it would die, and serve it right. All animals were idiotic, she thought, sheep above the rest, and deserved death and starvation and everything horrible. Why people wasted their time being sorry for them, and trying to help them and imagining they had feelings, she could not think. As for those odious societies for preventing cruelty being done to animals . . . at this moment a man with a gun across his shoulder came silent and brown out of the grey mist and faced her. She put forward her hand with a cry and touched his leather jerkin.

'I was lost,' she said. 'Are you the farmer?'

He said he was, and she told him of the sheep caught in barbed wire down by the canal. At once he plunged off at an angle with Nanette following. They slithered down a steep field and after dodging along beside the canal for quarter or half a mile came upon the animal in the same wretched plight as she had left it. He whipped out a pocket-knife and with a few business-like slashes cut it free. Before letting it go, he ran his hands all over it, deep in the wool.

'She's thin,' he said, looking up at Nanette. 'Must have been here days. Much obliged. D'you know where you are now?'

Nanette thanked him, said she did, and scurried off. Emma was waiting for her in an alarm that had been steadily growing. 'I thought you were drowned,' she said. 'I thought all sorts of things. It was so unlike you – more what Charity would have done.'

'That's why I did it,' answered Nanette, with an honesty that was one of her chief virtues.

'Well I'm glad you didn't kill it,' said Emma, shoving the *Venus* off the mud as she spoke. 'I thought at first when I saw you jump off with the knife you were going to do that.'

The long pound was broken by a flight of locks, different from other locks on the Bottom Road in that although of single width, they lay in pairs, and the motor-boat was allowed to pull the butty up the two short pounds. At the third and last pair of these locks a notable conversation took place.

'What does he look like?' asked Emma, referring to Wilfred.

Nanette hesitated. 'I can't remember very well,' she said.

'I thought he was an old friend of yours.'

'He's not an *old* friend,' replied Nanette evasively. 'That's to say, he is fairly old, but I haven't known him very long.'

'How long?'

'I met him – oh, about four weeks ago.'

'Do you mean to say you've only seen him once?'

'Well, yes; but we talked a great deal, for hours. He was awfully nice and I told him all about the canal. I don't see that it matters,' she added in answer to a certain expression on Emma's face.

Emma was silent until the *Venus* was moving out of the lock again and the long snubber uncoiling between the two boats. Then she said:

'*How* old?'

'I tell you, I forget. About forty or fifty I think.'

For the next two-and-a-half hours of winding water, Wilfred was uppermost in our minds. Nanette had suggested in her letter that if he could come we should meet him at half past seven in the bar of a public-house that was more like a private cottage so small and lonely was it. A battered sign swung outside it with the face of a negress just visible in ancient paint and the words *The Queen of Sheba* underneath. It was nearly the time agreed when we tied up.

'We must wash our faces,' said Nanette. 'We're still covered in coal from this morning.'

We splashed hot water hastily into the bowls and cleared the grime away from our faces and part of our necks. A black line ran round from ear to ear under our chins, and was softened off with towels. Becoming nervous, we tried to comb our hair.

'No, Nanette,' said Emma. 'Not lipstick. Nothing else. It strikes the wrong note.'

'But I look so awful like this,' cried Nanette, glaring in a mirror. 'I'm shining with soap; it's horrid.'

'Never mind. If we tart ourselves up he'll think it's a trap. Come on, we're late. No, you can't wear ear-rings. Nothing else. Just clean faces.' She dragged Nanette away from her box of tricks and out on to the tow-path.

We found Wilfred, our new mate, alone in the pub. He had been waiting over an hour for us. We wondered if he was always silent or if it was beer that made him like that. When he stood up he was tall with the unfleshy appearance of a vulture. His face was deeply lined, his hair was thin and grey. We talked on and on at him with a positive friendliness that soon wore us out. Apparently he listened to our chatter, though his large mournful eyes were fixed on the fire. It was difficult to know what he thought for he seldom answered.

15

Cleopatra took to Wilfred at once. She rode on his shoulder up Braunston locks, and chased after him from boat to boat, and closed her eyes in ecstasy whenever he touched her. Wilfred was an earnest student. He took the science of boating seriously. We had drawn him a diagram of a lock, speckled with misleading arrows, and with this in his pocket he undertook to lock-wheel for us. Now and again we caught a glimpse of him ahead of us standing on a lock-side with the paper fluttering in his hand, thoroughly puzzled. Sometimes he came tramping back to us.

'I can't make the gates open,' he would say. Or, stabbing at the diagram with a long white finger: 'I've found another *paddle*' – pronouncing the word loudly and fastidiously – 'just here, one you haven't marked. Is it all right to wind it up?'

We found ourselves drifting about in front of every lockgate while he sorted the matter out, for as yet he had not identified speed with boating, and was more concerned with getting everything exactly right. So he strode about above us attending with punctilious care to his new job, while the boats below lay slackly waiting, and we fretted and giggled. Each lock was a manoeuvre. He closed what he should close. He dropped what he had been told to drop. He watched with suffering eyes the water spouting out. He pushed open the gates and then without a glance at the boats, he picked up Cleopatra, set her

183

on his shoulder, and turned his face doggedly towards the next lock.

The tunnel at the top astonished him. 'Do we really go into this?' he asked, as we drew near it, lifting his eyebrows high above his great eyes with amazement.

'Of course we do,' said Nanette proudly. 'It takes forty minutes to reach the other end and sometimes the lights go out half-way through.'

But when he asked her exactly how long it was, the year it had been built, the depth of water inside it, and various details of engineering, she became peevish and said that she knew nothing about it except that it gave her forty minutes hell, and it was quite difficult enough trying to steer in the dark without having to answer questions she could hardly hear. In conclusion she gave him a thorough bumping and Wilfred relapsed into his usual silence. He sat inside the butty cabin with the light switched on. Nanette from outside, afraid she had been too short with him, peeped down into the small lighted cave and saw him sitting forward on the edge of the side-bed, his hands hanging loosely across his knees, enduring with an agonized patience the jolts and crashes and hideous scraping noises. His attitude was so restrained and so intense that she felt a flash of guiltiness for ever having written to him.

Buckby locks were kind to us. We met a pair of boats at the top of them. The steerer shouted out: 'There's another pair a-comin''; and so all the locks were ready and there was no need to send Wilfred on ahead.

Buckby is the town, the heaven-on-earth, of boaters. The little red-brick cottages are stuffed with ex-boaters or boaters' relations. Boaters' children race up and down the tow-path, boaters' dogs range about at large, and boaters' voices ring across the cut from one side to the other, the volume and pitch of them undiminished by a life on land. Here they retire; here they die and are buried; here they tie up and marry one another. A boater, on making a room his home instead of a cabin, changes none of his former habits. The walls are hung with the same brass knobs and lace and frilly plates. At first, perhaps, the additional space may trouble him, but he soon adapts himself and it soon silts up with bits of junk. The old women still stagger about with water-cans. The old men still totter out to wind a paddle for a passing relative.

Buckby, midway between London and Birmingham, is the receiving station for gossip. All the news drifts up against this filter, is gathered in, forked over, and tossed out into the stream again, fragment by fragment, as the boats pass on their way to the North or the South. News on the cut travels with lightening speed. Telephones and posts are out of date in comparison. The beer-boats carry it forward through the night, like runners with a flaming torch, and lock-keepers, toll-offices and Buckby all light their own match-sticks from it and brandish them till the cut is afire with winking signals. No accident can be kept a secret; no encounter is private; no conversation unrepeated. Courting can never be clandestine, and behaviour is hung out like a flag for all to see. A spotlight illuminates the life of a boating girl or boy from birth in a cabin to the grave at Buckby. But if, as occasionally happens, they break away from the cut to join the army or take a job in a factory, dark waters close above their heads. They step aside into an eternal silence, and the world has them.

'This is the way to take boats into a downhill lock,' we told Wilfred with prim authority. Nodding ferociously, he turned his full attention to this new lesson.

The locks at Buckby were deep. It was the job of the *Venus'* steerer to stay above while the boats were sinking down, in order to open the gates when the lock was empty. The drop that she then had to undertake from the lock-side to the cabin-top of the *Venus* was a formidable one. We all feared it. In wet weather, when the cabin-tops were slippery, it was even more alarming. The boats seemed to be lying at the bottom of a hole, a mile beneath; limbs felt brittle, and often we wavered on the lock-side pricking up our courage for the nightmare fall through space.

In an uphill lock the fear was reversed, for then it was necessary to stand on top of the cabin and leap up and out from the lock; and if the spring in the knees or the heave of the shoulders failed at the exact moment, there was always the possibility of falling back between the wall and the boat to be first crushed and afterwards drowned. This picture enlivened our minds every time we wriggled half-way up a lock-wall, with boots scrabbling for a purchase and arms taut, but only once was it almost made actual. Nanette had fetched out a box from the engine-hole and stood upon it to make herself taller. It broke as she sprang and she fell forward; luckily the gunwale brought her up standing, and she was saved though much frightened.

However, to-day there was no hesitation: Wilfred was watching. We threw ourselves down with deadly heroism, an example he did not follow, preferring to stroll ahead along the path from lock to lock till the last one.

'Wilfred,' shouted Emma. 'Keep the butty forward.' The paddles were wound; the boats were sinking down. Nanette was staring above her at a flock of birds. Wilfred zealously leapt upon the trailing rope and lashed it round a bollard. The boats continued to sink down and the rope snapped. Emma had once done the same thing herself. She ran up to him, vexation plain in her face.

'I'm sorry,' he said humbly.

'It seems so obvious,' she said. 'If the water-level drops a boat's bound to drop with it, and you can't hang a great heavy boat like that up as though it was a piece of washing.'

Wilfred laughed for the first time. He was caught by a perfect seizure of laughter, holding the broken length of rope in one hand and gasping. Emma was disconcerted. She eyed him angrily. She had thought of him as no laugher, and besides being surprised at his present spasm, found the reason for it both obscure and unhumorous.

186

'Can you splice?' she asked him.

'Naturally,' he said, his manner grave again. He spliced the rope together in the long pound and tidied it off with his penknife.

'Why,' said Emma. 'It's better than I could have done.'

'Naturally,' he said again, and she was troubled by his tone of voice. Wishing to put him at ease, she asked if he would care to clean the brasses, and at once he began to polish and rub as though his life depended on it. She watched his desperate industry kindly, and later remarked to Nanette that although he was a little slow in learning how to do things he certainly did his best.

'He may be slow,' said Nanette, 'but he never makes the same mistake twice, and he's awfully thorough.'

'But I'm afraid he isn't enjoying himself very much. He looks so worried all the time.'

'Oh, I think that's just his face,' said Nanette. 'I think he's one of those people who have a nice time without showing it.'

'He enjoyed busting that rope all right. He's a funny bird. I wish he'd *say* more. Do you think he thinks we're silly?'

'Oh no,' said Nanette. 'I expect he's shy; some men are. After all, it must be a lot different from being in charge of a battleship.'

'*Is* he in charge of a battleship?'

'Something like that, I expect,' said Nanette.

The day was cold and grey. We tackled the long pound half-buried under woollen scarves and extra jerseys, and steered with hands in our pockets and feet stamping. Grey willow branches swept the water on either side of us, and cheerless and ashen was the bleak pasture-land we threaded our way through, with grey herons trailing up from the rushy fringes and drifting listlessly away. Cloud, heavy and formless, hung between us and any hope of sunshine. The little cat, after walking nervously about the cabin-top and sneezing disapprovingly into the wind, retired below and went to sleep in front of the fire. Wilfred came back to the *Ariadne* and stood beside Nanette in the hatches until his anxiety made her anxious.

'Wilfred,' she said, breaking a long silence. 'It seems to me the butty's at an angle. What do you think? She's over to port, isn't she?'

He took a careful look and agreed.

'Could you shovel a bit of coal over?' said Nanette.

Wilfred shovelled. Every few minutes he looked up to ask if the butty was riding level yet.

'Not quite,' shouted Nanette. 'Bit more . . . bit more . . . that's about it I think.'

He scrambled out of the quicksands of coal, wiped his face and hands on a handkerchief and came back to stand in the hatches. Presently Nanette said:

'How extraordinary – look, she's listing to starboard.'

'There must be some water in the bilges,' said Wilfred, 'and it's running across from one side to the other. Shovelling won't put her straight. You want to pump. I suppose she's an old boat and leaks. And that reminds me – do you always sleep in wet beds?'

'I suppose we do. It's one of the things you get used to. Was my bed very wet?'

'Yes,' said Wilfred. 'It was the wettest bed I've ever slept in.'

'How about the bugs – did they bite you? I'm afraid my cabin's full of them; they can be very tiresome.'

'Bugs never bite me. Nor do mosquitoes, nor gnats, nor any kind of insect. I expect I'm too sour for them.'

Nanette dared not interpret this as a joke. She was reluctant also to suggest a spell of pumping, though the list was so pronounced that steering became more and more difficult. Wilfred seemed to appreciate this, for presently without a word to Nanette he tucked the ends of his trousers into his socks and waded through coal to the hand-pump. There he stayed, glued to his task, for the next half-hour. By the time the bilges were pumped dry the second tunnel, the one above Stoke locks, was in view. Wilfred asked if he might steer the butty through.

'If you like,' said Nanette, 'but it isn't easy. If we meet boats inside you must keep to the right-hand, and don't push the tiller out too far or you'll skin your knuckles.'

The *Venus* was just sliding her bows into the black mouth, Emma blowing a skirmish on her horn as she disappeared. Cleopatra stalked out of the cabin and leapt up on Wilfred's shoulder. Nanette switched on the headlight.

'Oh Lord,' she said. 'It's awfully feeble. I hope it lasts. We ought to have changed the batteries last night. Too late now.'

She planted the water-can squarely in the middle of the cabin-top and, unhitching the chimney-pot, laid it flat alongside the can.

'Why do you do that?' asked Wilfred. 'I'm going to have smoke in my face – is it necessary?'

'Yes it is. It only gets knocked down otherwise, because the walls slope over; you'll see.'

Wilfred turned up the collar of his coat and with bright owlish eyes directed his boat into obscurity. On the whole he did very well. Blinded during the first hundred yards or so, he rattled the boat about like dice in a box, bruising her against first one side and then the other. Then, with the head-lamp throwing a pale arc of light ahead and his own sight strengthening, he struck a fair middle course and only scraped against the wall twice more on the whole run. He seemed to have an instinct for steering; his hand on the tiller was alive and nervy.

When they emerged into daylight Nanette scrambled out of the cabin and praised him. He handed the tiller back to her and lowered his eyes. For a moment she thought he was going to burst into one of his gales of laughter, but instead he lit a cigarette. The sombre lines of his face were just beginning to be clouded in a stubble of dark hair, and the result was absurd and at the same time intimidating. He swivelled his awful gaze round the *Ariadne*.

'Where's the kitten?' he said.

It had happened at last: the kitten was gone. Cleopatra was not on board.

'She jumped on my shoulder,' said Wilfred, 'just as we were going into the tunnel.'

The top lock of the flight was ready for us and the gates were standing open. As the butty-boat overhauled the *Venus*, Nanette screamed aloud to Emma:

'Cleopatra's missing. She must have drowned in the tunnel.'

We were all sickened.

'I suppose she lost her footing, poor beast, with all that bumping,' said Wilfred, 'or else I kicked her overboard in the dark. Nothing we can do.'

'I wonder how long she swam,' said Emma.

'Perhaps she was squashed.'

'Poor Cleopatra.'

'Poor Charity,' said Nanette.

Soberly we closed the gates and drew the paddles. The thought of the cat we had scolded so often, left behind in the icy heart of the tunnel, attempting with wild alarm to save her life by swimming as we had once before seen her doing – this depressed us horribly.

'She must be dead by now,' said Wilfred, as a comfort. But in our minds she was alive all that day, fighting the water, and some of her terror she left behind to haunt us.

We met Sam Stevens above the fourth lock, coming up. Sam had loaded with us at Limehouse, a fortnight before.

'You've been quick,' we shouted.

He inclined his head and we saw him shoot a quick glance towards Wilfred who was walking on.

'We lost our mate on the Bottom Road,' said Emma in explanation.

She told him about the bridge, and then about the sinking episode. We felt he was nearly our friend, and sensed that entertaining stories were the hoops of iron that would grapple him to our souls. Our boats were waiting in one lock while his boats, directed by Mrs. Stevens and family, worked their way up through the lock below. A swarm of his youngsters, chiefly boys, over-ran the lock-side armed with windlasses. We watched them as we talked. Sam leaned over a paddle, his eyes for his family and his ears for us. He was a lean middle-aged man and handsome in a useful weathered way, with clumsy boots disguising the leap and balance of a tiger. 'Oh-ah,' he said now and again, and he listened intently.

'So he's your new chap then?' he said at the end. He was not quite clear about Wilfred.

'He's my uncle,' said Nanette quickly as we jumped down aboard the boats.

Emma jogged her arm. To lie was an error. Lies on the cut had a short life. 'Why did you say that? He's sure to find out.'

'Then we'll have to tell everyone he's my uncle. Wilfred,' she said, when we caught him up at the next lock, 'you've got to be my uncle.'

'Very well,' said Wilfred.

He said he would like to steer the motor-boat into a lock. Emma handed the *Venus* over to him and walked on ahead. The gates were lying open as the Stevens had left them. She sat herself on the end of a beam, her legs dangling over the full and gently lapping water. Her mood was abstracted and delicately morbid. Wilfred brought the *Venus* in on the opposite side a touch too fast but with undeniable skill – indeed, with a hint of flashiness. He bent and cast off the tow-rope as the butty came racing afterwards.

Emma, to honour him, lifted her hands and clapped them above her head. As she did so the bows of the butty hit the other end of the gate on which she was sitting with a resounding smack, knocking it flush back against the wall, and catapulting her forward to fall a yard or so in advance of the onrushing *Ariadne*.

Ages of terror engulfed her. She touched in a few moments the very nerve of frenzy. Nothing on earth could check that crushing speed. She saw Nanette at the tiller as she fell, a mile, a world away, her face round and shocked, without a bollard or even a tow-path at hand, surrounded by water, powerless to save her. She was Cleopatra and dying. Water smothered over her head. She sank through it like lead into darkness. And sinking, drowning, her blazing mind explained to her the horror of suffocation, trapped underneath the boat. For air, for the mercy of a blow on the head and death by crushing she kicked with all her might and madness and burst above the surface to find the black bows towering over her. Escape by swimming was out of the question. She had just time to fling her arms across the stone edge of the lock and utter one animal whimper of dread, when heaven snatched her up by the scruff of the neck and the ghastly machine of destruction glided into the lock beneath her heels.

Heaven was Wilfred. He set her down like a rescued rat on the lock-side and looked at her critically. Emma had a mild fit of hysterics. The butty crashed at full speed against the farther gates. Nanette, expensively thrilled, came racing up to say she had *never* been so frightened.

Dripping with tears and canal-water, her teeth chattering, hair plastered down her cheeks, Emma declared that no one could have steered a motor-boat into a lock better; here she broke into laughter, changed it to tears, and was sternly taken in hand by Wilfred.

'Change your clothes,' he said, gripping her arm until she noticed the pain, 'and blow your nose.' Then he let the water out of the lock and opened the gates. Before setting the motor-boat ahead, he handed down a flask of whisky into the butty cabin.

'Drink a lot,' he said. 'Drink about half the bottle. Yes,' he cried, shouting down her protest in a loud bullying voice. 'I've got more of it, pints of it. Drink it up. Do as I say.'

And back he went to his job of managing the *Venus*. As Emma swallowed his whisky she heard him mournfully whistling. Feeling as though she was recovering from a long illness, her strength sapped all away, she crept out into the butty hatches beside Nanette, and together we watched our callow mate take the *Venus* into the last lock as nicely as a gentleman might sheath his sword. His expression was as lugubrious as ever, but there was no overlooking a certain masterful triumph about him. Emma winced when she remembered how that morning she had bade him clean the brasses. Nanette thought of him shovelling coal. How had we dared to treat him so, he, a hero and a natural boater?

Later that afternoon he said to Emma: 'How much do you weigh?'

'Ten stone,' she answered. 'Thank you *very* much for saving my life.'

'Bloody silly place to sit,' he snarled at her.

'Well, it's lucky you were there or I should be dead by now.'

'No you wouldn't. If I hadn't been there, you'd have been steering the boat not playing the fool on a gate. It all works out.'

'You must be very strong.'

He waved her reverence aside. 'No, indeed I'm not, not a bit. On the contrary. It nearly gave me a heart-attack fishing you out. I've never known a girl so heavy. Solid, right the way through.'

'It's muscle,' she murmured.

'It's unwomanly,' said he.

This killing blow sent Emma rushing back to her best friend for contradiction. 'Oh, Nanette, I'm not. It isn't true,' she cried.

Nanette sparkled with malice. 'Don't ask me. Wilfred's a man – he ought to know.'

193

Emma regarded her figure inch by inch in a hand-mirror, moaning. 'He's old and out of date,' she said, 'Oh, how awful to be unwomanly. But I'm not, I'm not. Nanette, am I? What do you think I can do?'

'Nothing,' said Nanette complacently. 'It's the way you're born. Do you think you ought to leave Wilfred alone on the motor? After all, he's only a new hand and it's getting dark.'

'I'm not going near him,' said Emma, nearly in tears again. 'Let him get on with it by himself.'

So Wilfred got on with it to the extent of running headlong into a pair of stationary boats tied on a corner. They were lying singly along the outside bank, and the impact was considerable. So was the subsequent swearing. Lanterns bobbed along the tow-path. Blame was tossed with vigour from side to side. We had come into contact with boats of a different company. They were made of wood and our *Venus*, guided by our Wilfred, had stove a hole in the bows of the leading one.

'You ain't got no business. . .'

We all said it, with variations, Wilfred perhaps the most forcefully. There was a mist rising off the face of the water, as it so often did at the end of the day; a cold and feathery twilight was dropping down to meet it, first distorting breath of night, when the air hums and dances as though with a million gnats, and the eye, widening, chases amongst it for the remnant of shrinking day. There was heavy cloud, there was no moon, there were no lights on the boats – justification poured out. It was not a regular tying place: this was a trump card.

'You've no business to be tied here at all,' cried Nanette.

But inspection proved a better point against us: the *Venus* for the second time had lost her bows fender. There was her wicked prow, naked, and above it the rotten holes where the staples had torn themselves out. This little slip later cost our Company a good deal of money. For the moment we were

worsted. Our enemies swung their lanterns over the *Venus*'
bows, and there was nothing more to say.

Emma, her spirits fully restored, skipped back along the
centre-planks. For if Wilfred was a bungler, his opinion of her
lost its value. She ousted him from the *Venus*' deck.

'I think perhaps I'd better steer,' she said.

Half an hour later we tied in pitch darkness to some trees
growing on the right-hand side of the cut, opposite to the tow-
path. It was an unsatisfactory tie-up but we had no choice. A
certain amount of philandering went on with the branches
before we succeeded in making ourselves semi-fast. Wilfred
caught hold of a handful of twigs, insisted they were tugging
him overboard, and let go. The boats drifted out and were
shafted back into position by Nanette. Emma switched on one
headlight in defiance of black-out laws and arbitrarily pointed
out a bough for Wilfred to capture, at the same time snatching
a nearby one herself. Wilfred declared his was out of reach; she
bade him stretch, the boats drifted, Nanette shafted. Every
blade of grass and crooked bud showed up glaringly clear, and
so did Wilfred. He struggled for a few minutes in the bright
beam, his head amongst a forest of irritating twigs, and then
with a curse flung himself towards the shore. He missed the
bank, stung his hands in a bed of nettles, wet his shoes,
splashed his trousers with mud, but had us tied to the trunks
of two stout trees within five minutes, and the operation
concluded. Even so, mud prevented us from lying in close
and we had to use a gang-plank to take us ashore for the drink
we felt we deserved.

We were tied at the foot of a garden belonging to an hotel,
and had to squash our way across lawns and flower-beds and
round gravel paths before finding the front door and the big
empty bar beyond it. Nanette was inclined to be timid. Copper
warming-pans hung on the walls; the chairs were upholstered
in an apple-green fabric.

'Aren't we a little shabby for this place?' she said.

Shabby was an understatement: we were in a state of flamboyant filth. Wilfred looked particularly villainous. To save his own, he had borrowed a jacket much too small for him and his bony wrists hung out of the sleeves. His trousers were torn at the knee and his hair stood on end.

'Rubbish,' said he, pushing Nanette in the small of the back. 'They're lucky to have us; we give it tone, distinction, everything it hasn't got.' He strode noisily across the floor.

'There's something *about* Wilfred,' said Nanette, following. 'A sort of *presence*. . .'

There was something else about him, too, we had never suspected. After a drink and five minutes conversation with the bar-maid he came grimly across to us carrying six eggs.

'Did you see that?' whispered Emma. 'He vamped her. . .'

'He wheeled her just the same way he does a lock,' said Nanette.

He gave us beer as though it was medicine, and stood over us to see we drank it down at a gulp. Meekly we swallowed as many doses as he thought were good for us, and then allowed ourselves to be shepherded back down the garden slopes on to the boats. It was Wilfred who broke the six eggs into an omelette, who finished the week's ration of cheese and who, insisting on coffee, made it himself so strong and black it almost had to be eaten. And it was Wilfred who, doling cigarettes out to the crew after supper, suggested a game of poker.

'We don't know how to play,' said Nanette.

'You'll soon learn,' said Wilfred. 'The rules are easy.'

So with hatches tight shut and the red and white check curtains drawn across the port-hole and the stove a furnace, we took our first lessons in poker. After half an hour the lights faded out of existence and the hurricane lamp was lit. Jersey by jersey we relieved ourselves of the overpowering heat and even in shirt-sleeves sweated the dirt out of us in streams. Whisky we remembered afterwards as a dim accompaniment, but only the cards were alive and we were in a coma.

'How much money,' said Nanette, hours later, 'has Wilfred won?'

'All of it,' said Emma, turning the cocoa tin where we kept it upside down. 'He'll have to lend us some to-morrow to buy the food. He did play well, didn't he?'

'I don't remember,' said Nanette.

Smoke drifted away through the open hatches into a night that was starry and windless. An owl somewhere hooted its single note, over and over again. Otherwise there was no noise. The country was still, stretching out its flat miles around us. The boats rocked. The water shone darkly.

16

Waking next morning, Emma remembered having once said that Nanette should learn to fend for herself. She therefore stirred her up with one foot until Nanette responded with a muffled: 'Leave me alone.'

'You can get the breakfast to-day. It'll do you good. Go on.'

After a long silence, Nanette said: 'All right. But I won't light the Primus.'

'Well I shan't. You've got to learn, Nanette. Have some guts.'

The result of this would-be invigorating remark was disastrous. In a few minutes the Primus burst into a pillar of fire. The cabin reeked of scorching varnish and paraffin smoke. Risking her eyebrows, Nanette snatched up the bundle of flame and, bounding into the hatches, flung it as far from her as possible. The blaze was extinguished in a muddy splash, and that was the end of our Primus.

'You silly mug,' wailed Emma. 'Why did you throw it away?'

'The boat would have been on fire in a moment. Blame yourself – I warned you. You shouldn't try to force my nature.'

'Blow your nature. You pumped too soon, that's all. And why didn't you chuck some water *over* it?'

'I lost my head,' said Nanette. 'It doesn't matter, don't fuss. We've got an oil-stove.'

'Yes, and it takes twenty minutes to boil a kettle.'

'All right; never mind. What's twenty minutes, what's a Primus? Stop killing yourself with worry. I burned my hands – you might consider that.'

'It was my Primus; it was MY Primus,' said Emma, more and more depressed.

'Oh well,' said Nanette. 'Now you're just being sloppy.'

Later on in the morning it started raining in a way so hesitating that every minute we thought it was going to stop. Wilfred put on a sou'wester. At Fenny Stratford we stocked up with tinned milk, borrowing twelve and six from Wilfred in order to do so. The woman in the pub asked kindly after our cat, and we said it was dead. She offered to give us one of her own white kittens, and danced it along the counter to show how pretty it was. We were doubtful, and asked her to keep it for a time.

'Charity may not want another cat,' said Emma. 'She was specially fond of Cleopatra. We'll be passing again in a week; we'll let you know then.'

'No hurry,' she said. 'I've got plenty of 'em and they keep comin'.'

Wilfred appeared in the doorway, an arresting figure with his sou'wester and his bristling ravaged face. He called the landlady 'Madam' and begged her for a drink. She called him 'Sir' and had to refuse. It was out of hours, she was sorry, she dared not oblige him. He was wet, he was cold, cried Wilfred, his eyes afire – she saw how he was; he touched himself proudly on the chest with the tips of his fingers – he had been working half the night. Hours? What were hours in such a state and on a canal?

Oh dear, she was sorry; she understood, she knew just how he felt. But there it was. In the end she sold him three bottles of beer and came running after him into the rain to give him a fourth. He lifted his sou'wester with a striking courtesy and she never forgot him.

' 'Is h'eyes 'aunted me,' she said to us the next time we saw her.

The birds for some reason were singing loudly. The rain was very soft and misty. Nanette steered the butty with an umbrella held above her head, while Emma peeled potatoes and Wilfred was happy on the *Venus*. He blew his horn often and was particular about giving signals to Nanette, inventing special signs not only to tell her when boats were coming, but to indicate a bridge or a corner or dab-chicks or a heron, or indeed, anything. Nanette said it made it much more interesting as she never knew what he meant, though she nodded and waved her umbrella.

A pair of swans burst out of the cloud behind us and swinging low over our heads landed a hundred yards in front of the boats in a flurry of white feathers and foam. Nanette hopped with pleasure.

'Lovely,' she cried.

Suddenly we were filled with jubilation. Our spirits rocketed up. We were nearly home. In two days we should be back in London. We were Columbus returning with coal for treasure. That our friends, for whose ears we were already preparing boastful stories, might not be agog to greet us, might indeed hardly have noticed our absence – this had not occurred to us. We felt we had been away a short lifetime and that, while we had waded through the deep waters of experience, they must have done nothing but shade their eyes and watch for us. We were soon to be disabused, but at that moment and for the next two days we were outsize in our own minds, and very nice it felt.

As Leighton Buzzard lock came into sight we saw a lock-wheeler sitting astride a beam. Wilfred failed at first to understand the significance of a lock-wheeler. Nanette shouted at the top of her voice that boats were coming and we must wait. At once Wilfred went hard astern.

'Emma, quick – pull up the snubber, he'll have it in his blades in a moment. Neutral,' she screamed to Wilfred. 'Go into neutral' but her voice was drowned in the whining of gears. Emma flew up to the bows and hauled in the sopping snubber hand over fist.

'You mustn't go hard astern like that,' she said to Wilfred when the snubber was heaped safely aboard the deck. Nanette had succeeded in running the butty on to the mud and the *Venus* was drifting back alongside the *Ariadne*.

'But isn't that the way you stop a boat? You told me it was.'

'So it is; but don't you see, if there's lots of rope slack in the water the propeller blades pick it up, and I can't tell you what it's like to have a snubber in the blades.'

Nanette was amusing herself by feeding a drove of ducks off the stern-end. They came crowding greedily round, wagging their rumps. One of them was larger than the rest, the colour of toffee and very fat. Wilfred, fastening on this one, began to tempt it nearer and nearer with a crust of bread. As soon as it came within reach, he clapped it up out of the water and planted it down in the butty hatches. The other ducks swam round in the mist exclaiming in loud quacks, while the prisoner craned its neck over the edge in some astonishment.

'Supper,' said Wilfred in an off-hand voice, as though he was accustomed to picking up his food wherever he might.

'Surely you aren't going to kill it?'

'Of course I'm going to kill it. What, waste that lovely bird in hard times like these? Not for a moment. Decent grub tonight, young ladies.'

'We can't cook it,' said Nanette. 'The oven doesn't work.'

'Then we'll toast it on forks, and if it's rather underdone – why, never mind. It's richer when it's raw.'

'You won't get me to pluck it,' said Emma. The sensible creature looked up at her with its bright eyes, inquisitive but not in the least alarmed. 'I think it's rather mean to kill it,' she added, not quite sure whether Wilfred was joking or not.

He leaned towards her and said in a low voice: '*Let's* be mean to animals – they can't be mean to us.'

She was startled and suddenly rather angry. 'No, I won't let you,' she cried, and scrambling the duck up in her arms, dumped it anyhow over the side. Outraged at her roughness, it at once began to scold and fuss and flap its wings.

'You see,' said Wilfred moodily. 'No thanks – a waste of kindness. It only hates you now.'

The boats were riding out past us. The ducks were scattered. We hastened to our places. The steerer of the motor-boat was grinning.

'Put you in prison for that,' he called out.

'Wilfred,' said Emma, puzzled by him as she always was. 'Are you cruel?'

'Horribly,' said he, and gave her such a piercing glance that she believed him.

In half an hour the days of long quiet pounds were over. From then on the land went up and up with a lock every ten or fifteen minutes to Tring Summit, and then down and down to London. The bicycle was constantly out on the tow-path and meals were hurried and broken. Nanette and Wilfred forked up their tinned stew as they steered. Emma balanced hers in a saucepan across the handle-bars and wolfed it down in three minutes while a lock was emptying.

We fell back on the old routine of wheeling four locks each, taking similar turns in steering the butty and the motor. Wilfred disliked the butty, saying she was a silly boat with no proper feelings, a regular bore of a boat. She was heavy on the turn and, being without a motor, answered more slowly to the tiller. The *Venus*, on the other hand, responded to a fraction, and Wilfred wooed her like a lover, displaying a sweetness and tact he possibly kept for boats. Nanette, who was never very fond of responsibility, preferred to steer the more prosaic butty, so by arrangement Wilfred took over her turns on the *Venus* and both of them were satisfied.

Through lack of personal conversation and the rhythm of team-work, we felt by the middle of the afternoon that Wilfred was part of our outfit, and forgot to be ill at ease with him. The mist blew into our faces and damped our hands but never became a downpour. Wilfred continued to protect his head with a sou'wester, the strings of it tied in a bow beneath his chin, but allowed the rest of himself to be gradually wetted. As for us, we were heated with exercise and found the soft drizzle refreshing. We went without jackets altogether and rolled up the sleeves of our jerseys to feel the cool rain fan our forearms. We were happy, near enough London to be in home waters again, far enough out to have fields still round us and hills rising in the distance.

Now and again we ran into lock-keepers patrolling on their bicycles, and as they helped us wind the paddles, they gave us the latest bulletins of war. During the next two years, we heard, in their dialect, momentous news. In parts of England desolate and green the names of battles, retreats and massacres were shouted down to us. It was they who told us of slaughter in foreign towns when our summer was at its strength, blistering the boats with its heat, bleaching our hair, dazzling our eyes with grasses and blowing seed and poppies. We could be neither frightened nor sorrowful, though we tried. Sunshine flushed our immediate minute with its ardour, and horror was a quaintness, a distant gong in our ears. In autumn and winter our chattering hands were busy with ropes, cold and wet; we were stunned by the noise of falling water, giddy with falling leaves; lock-keepers' voices were blown by the wind into rare tunes, and we understood nothing but joy.

Here we were, on a Tuesday afternoon in March, creeping over the miles towards London, and at half past three Wilfred broke the butty-tiller. We were silent. There were, after all, a good many other things he might have done and had not. He might have lost a windlass, he might have knocked a water-can overboard, or put the butty on the sill or made a host of other mistakes. In two days he had pushed a hole in someone else's boat, broken only one rope and the tiller. We were bound to consider this a moderate price for his services.

By accident he had been left in charge of the butty he so detested. We had no loop of string fastened to the cabin-top, as most boats had, in which to catch the end of the tiller, having found that string was inadequate. On going into a lock, we always lifted the heavy wooden tiller bodily out from the helm and stood it upright in the hatches, quite out of harm's way. Not Wilfred. Perhaps he forgot, or perhaps he was impatient, and we only noticed his omission when we heard the tiller crack in half with a noise like a gunshot. For the helm had been forced round by the inrush of water when the paddles at the far end were lifted, and the long branch of the tiller, swinging across with it against the lock wall, snapped like a twig. It was to prevent exactly this that a tiller was hooked prisoner in a loop of string or lifted clear. We brought out the spare one. Wilfred refused to be sorry. He had never cared for the butty and had the feeling, we knew, that a broken tiller served it right. We managed not to reproach him, except for one remark of Nanette's. She said:

'It isn't money you're costing us, Wilfred, but our reputations.'

'On the contrary,' he answered equably, 'you should be grateful. I'm giving you one. Just wait till they find out I'm not your uncle.'

It was an hour later, just below Marsworth locks, that Nanette unusually distinguished herself. She bicycled into the cut.

The path was steep and stony, dropping at a sharp angle down from the bridge. There had always been a certain incompatibility between Nanette and bicycles. She had gone ahead to lock-wheel and on discovering boats, came pelting back to warn us. We saw her shoot into sight over the bridge, her mouth open, bicycle at full wobble, one arm waving; the next moment her front tyre skidded amongst the loose boulders and with a cry she flew to one side and disappeared with her bicycle into the cut.

We could do nothing. We were several hundred yards away and in mid-water. However, it was not dangerous, being only a few feet deep where she fell and more a muddy grave than a watery one. We watched her scramble up the bank dripping with mud and weeds, and dragging the awkward bicycle after her by its handle-bars.

'Are you hurt?' shouted Emma, as soon as she was near enough to be heard.

Nanette shook her head.

Wilfred, from the deck of the motor-boat, called out that he thought we ought to tie up. We tied up. It had been a day full of mistakes and was then only half past four. Nanette said she thought a little whisky would help her condition, so Wilfred gave her the last of it.

'You girls,' he said, 'are too frivolous to be alive. I never knew anything like it. Bridges bang you on the head; bicycles carry you into the cut. Have you no stability?'

'Well, only Nanette would bicycle into the cut. I do think that's the silliest thing I ever heard of.'

'You,' said Wilfred, 'prefer to be bounced in?'

'That's an unfriendly thing to say. Why are you sometimes so unfriendly, Wilfred?'

'You misunderstand me,' said Wilfred. 'I'm only trying to learn. You forget – all this is new to me. I'm a student.'

He then amazed her by constructing a very neat fender out of old ends of rope and lashing it to the bows of the *Venus* so firmly that little short of dynamite would ever dislodge it. Nanette, in warm dry woolies with a whisky-flush in her cheeks, presently joined us. With some respect, we watched Wilfred's knobbly hands at work, and after a time found that he was also being watched from the tow-path by an American airman, also respectful. Wilfred went on with his knots and hammering, and the khaki trousers stayed where they were beside us. When the fender was fixed, the American said to Wilfred:

'Allow me to congratulate you, sir.'

'Thank you,' said Wilfred, hammer in hand. His chin presented a marked contrast to the clean-shaven one addressing him. His clothes too were very different.

'If you'll pardon the liberty, I'd like to ask if you find this sort of life sufficiently stimulating? Isn't it just a little slow?'

'I'm used to it,' said Wilfred simply. 'I suppose it's in my blood. Flying, of course, would be quicker. It must be very interesting to fly.'

'Oh, I'm not a flyer, I stay down on the ground. This is the first time I've visited England, but I certainly hope it isn't the last. I think your canals are very beautiful. Would you do me the favour of letting me photograph you and your family?' There was a camera hanging round his neck.

'You're very kind,' said Wilfred. He put an arm round each of us, across our shoulders. 'These are my two wives.'

'Is that so? Tell me, is that strictly in order?'

'It's one of the canal's oldest prerogatives,' Wilfred answered. 'Not a very happy one.'

The American recorded this ancient custom with his camera and said he was much obliged.

'It's very under-bred of you to snigger,' said Wilfred, once he had gone. 'England's ashamed of you.'

'Wilfred, he believed you.'

'It does him credit. I thought his politeness was charming and highly civilized, which is more than anyone could say of you.'

'It wasn't very civilized of you to pull his leg.'

'I wasn't pulling his leg. I was telling him the sort of things he wanted to hear, and that *is* being civilized.'

There was no point in playing poker that evening, since neither Emma nor Nanette had any more money to lose. There were no valuables aboard except an alarm clock and

Nanette's watch which had recently stopped. Wilfred said that since these were worth practically nothing at all it would be better to have a game of darts in the local. And this is what we did.

17

'B ut what was he like?' asked Charity.

She had come back to us with no bits of silver in her head and her death postponed indefinitely. We saw her leaning over a bridge above the Cow Roast lock, and could hardly believe our eyes. Nothing had warned us, no telegram, no letter. There she suddenly was, at half past ten in the morning, unmistakably Charity even in the distance. Her blue jersey had been through the wash and was brighter. She began to wave the moment we came into sight. We waved back, amazed, and blew the horns before we were near enough to shout.

Her hair, we saw, as the boats came closer, had been improved in the same way as her jersey; she was clean all over, like a birthday present only just unwrapped. We felt in comparison much crumpled, as though we had slept badly for a good many nights in succession, which was not the case – we were asleep, always, the second we laid our heads down and sometimes before. We called out, but she answered nothing, only smiling. She allowed the boats to pass right into the locks, perhaps to remind herself of how it was done, before catching up her bag and running down, her face filled with pleasure. Under one arm she carried a lute.

'Back again,' she said, leaping aboard the coal and flinging her bag away in any direction, plainly as glad as it was possible to be.

'This is Wilfred,' said Nanette, hurriedly pointing towards him.

Wilfred bowed. He had been standing erect on the gunwale of the *Venus* like a finger of rock. His face, which he had left unshaved, was by this time heavily disguised in bristle and his thoughts, never very plain to us, were concealed by the same mask.

Charity had cooked us a cake and wrapped it in her clean underclothes with a bunch of violets, picked by herself that morning, on top. Violets, a lute, and a home-made cake – these were the devices on Charity's coat-of-arms. The flowers we put in a jam-jar; the cake we ate that evening, and eating it told her of how Wilfred had been sent for, and had come, and had saved Emma's life and taught us poker and broken the butty-tiller.

'But,' said Charity, 'what was he *like*?'

'We don't know,' said Nanette. 'He never told us. We never even knew if he liked us. We rather think he didn't.'

'Of course I hardly saw him and he never said a word to me except he was glad I hadn't broken my head, but I had the feeling he was a real clown. He had the face of a clown – those melancholy eyes, just like a clown's.'

'Oh no, you're quite wrong,' cried Nanette. 'He wasn't at all a funny man, was he Emma? He was the most serious man I've ever met, in fact.'

Emma was silent. After a time she said: 'I don't know. I'm not sure. I believe Charity's right. I believe he thought the whole thing was one enormous joke from start to finish – the boats, us, everything. I think he must have been laughing all the time.'

There was a three minute silence while we thought of our sad Wilfred, now departed.

'Oh dear,' said Nanette at last. 'Then he did make fools of us. How serious we must have seemed. We're too young, that's what the trouble is. How awful.'

So Wilfred, who had disconcerted us at our first meeting, continued to disconcert us even after he was gone. He had left the boats at Berkhamsted, a few locks after Charity's return. Without a word, he packed his canvas bag and climbed out of the cabin with it at Berkhamsted lock. We protested at once.

'Don't go. Not now. Stay a little longer – till to-night, till to-morrow. You can't go straight away.'

This precipitation of departure brought the usual rush of easy emotion to our heads. A tie was being broken. We tried to delay the passing of any portion of our lives – for we still imagined we lost, not gained, the minutes – and begged him wait till the morning.

Naturally Wilfred never changed his mind. It was convenient, he said, to get a train from Berkhamsted; they ran every half hour or so, and the station was nearby. Then he shook each of us by the hand, without smiling but with a warm civility. We thanked him for coming. We rather over-thanked him.

'It was my pleasure,' he said, looking for a moment like a drawing of God by William Blake, and after that he went away.

The locks came thick and fast, not in flights but singly, one after another. We met a number of boats coming up loaded from the docks and most of the locks were ready for us. Charity stayed aboard the *Venus*, swinging her legs from the cabin-top, waving to all the passing boaters and anyone else who seemed interested. She was exuberant as we had never seen her before, and when men called out and whistled from the dark interiors of work-shops, it was to Charity, not us. We enjoyed her without envy. And if we felt like drudges and dull beside her, we were too pleased at having her back to mind. The sun fluttered in and out like a flag in the wind; the boats careered along.

'But how did you know where to find us?'

'I worked it out in my head. I guessed you'd be somewhere near the Cow Roast, though I really thought you'd have tied there last night. I asked the lock-keeper, and he said no, you hadn't been through, so I waited, and then you came.'

'What did you do at home?' asked Emma, thirsting for descriptions of voluptuous luxury.

'I slept nearly all the time. And I kept thinking about the boats. Whenever it rained I imagined you both, and when it was a sunny day I thought how lovely to be on the cut, and longed to be back.'

'And is your head really all right?'

'Oh, perfectly, yes. It was only bruised, not cracked. But the doctor said I was lucky, I must have a thick skull.'

'Nanette thought you were going to die.'

'Oh well, I suppose I might have done, but there, I didn't. I don't believe you've scrubbed the hatches once since I've been away. Do let me steer. Really, how nice it all is.'

A main road ran along beside the cut and we saw our first red double-decker bus, straight from London. On the other side was a railway, and trains like whirlwinds tore past us, loaded with people, and were gone in a few seconds taking their noise with them and leaving their smoke behind. It took two hours by train to travel from London to Birmingham; for us it was a five-day journey and we reckoned the distance in miles. We were back amongst the houses – old ones left over from the village days, and new suburban horrors trying to look at ease under those ancient and dignified trees that had not yet been cut down, though they were surely doomed. We passed football-fields and playing-grounds, and heard from open factory windows the magnified cheerfulness of 'Music While You Work'.

So this was industry, forgotten by us amongst our damp hills, and now remembered: people in bulk, work in the mass; streams of men and women across the bridges at six o'clock; the green or the white overalls with initials on the pocket; the bent heads, the grimy window, the sudden face; the thermos and breath of fresh air at half past four; packing-cases cluttered on the little wharfs; the blast of music, the flash of machinery. And the days having names again, like Monday or Tuesday, instead of being to-morrow or yesterday.

The web of London, with its million cries and movements, took us back. On the whole we were glad. Deserts turn lonely after a time, and cows as companions seem inadequate. Besides, we knew that after plunging into the hurly-burly for a few days we should then withdraw again into our deserts and find them twice as agreeable for the change. The slowness of cows, lately an irritation, would then seem philosophic. We needed our contrasts and were given them, lucky and undeserving creatures that we were, as regular as clockwork.

We arrived at our destination, a paper factory, at half past two in the afternoon. Boats, just emptied, were moving off. We took their place. The little concrete wharf was inches thick in coal-dust and a good half of it was piled mountain high with actual coal. Above our heads Harry leaned out of his cage, a box that trundled to and fro very much like the contraption in old-fashioned drapers for carrying the money between counter and cash-desk.

' 'Ullo girls,' he said.

'Harry, can you unload us straight away? We're in a hurry. We want to get home.'

'Can't do nothing till Leslie comes back. Did you have a nice trip?'

'Yes thank you. Where's Leslie?'

'I dunno,' said Harry, ' 'e didn't say.'

Leslie was his mate who worked on the ground, directing the grab that Harry raised and lowered, and shovelling the coal into preparatory piles. It was a long job at the best of times. We tied our ropes to the steel rings, rolled back the side-cloths and threw ashore the planks. Leslie was still absent.

'Oh Harry! Where *is* he? What's he doing?'

213

'Dunno,' said Harry, comfortably watching us.

'Couldn't you start without him?' We stared upwards, exasperated.

'Can't do that. What would the union say?'

'Who's going to tell the union?'

'Wouldn't be right,' said Harry.

'I'm starving,' said Nanette. 'We haven't had anything to eat yet and it's nearly three o'clock.'

So we had a meal of dinner and tea together, and half-way through it Leslie came back, and they began to unload us. We ate in relaxed positions, tossing tins as we opened them out through the hatches into the cut. Our clothes showed the wear and tear of a hard journey. Our boots were falling to bits, our trousers frayed, our socks in tatters. The cabin had never looked so slovenly, and the books in the shelves were mildewed. Charity said the thing that was worrying us all.

'I suppose Cleopatra's dead,' she said in her clear cool voice.

We were so ashamed and miserable, all we could do was nod.

'I guessed it,' she said, 'as soon as I came aboard. I think I knew it would happen really when I left her. Don't tell me,' she added quickly as Nanette opened her mouth, 'anything about it. I don't want to know. Poor Pussy's dead,' she sang, picking up the lute. 'Poor . . . Pussy's . . . dead. . . .'

We glanced above her bent head at one another, much relieved. No tears from Charity, not a single reproach. Only a doleful dirge and a perfectly wicked look when we met her eye. Like Wilfred, she was a puzzle. We could never make out if she was as hard as a nut, or as soft as a plum, or something in between like a cabbage.

There was a knocking on the side of the cabin. Emma put her head outside.

'Tilly . . .!'

We dragged her in. 'I can't wait,' she said at once. 'Well, just a cup of tea then, if it isn't too hot.'

214

She was our teacher, our original friend. We had to tell her all about our first trip without her; exaggerating, contradicting, repeating, we poured it out, a triumphant pæan, for here we were at the end of it. She had heard of Wilfred.

'How the news travels.' We whispered he was not an uncle. Oh, she knew that too. She knew everything. She knew of Charity's accident.

'I was so worried when I heard. Are you all right now? Someone seems to hurt herself every day. One girl I was teaching broke her ankle, another one strained her heart. You must be careful. Are you careful? Are you all strong enough to do it? Of course it's more a case of balance really. I feel it's my fault if you break yourselves up.' She sat swallowing down her tea on the edge of the coal-box, as bright as a bird, as smart and spry as a robin. We assured her we were strong, steady-footed, had never felt better in our lives; no one could fool us now, we said – we were wily, watchful, old hands at the game. How were her new pupils?

'So-so,' said Tilly. 'They drive me nearly mad at times, but they'll learn or they'll leave, one or the other, and I shan't know which till the end of the trip. There they are.' She cocked her head. We heard the patter of an engine. 'It's too bad we can't tie up together,' she said, 'but I must push on. If I don't work 'em till they drop they think it's a soft job.'

She was just the same, taut as a wire, spilling energy over with every word. The same bell-bottoms, the same peaked cap, the same ear-rings – the same Tilly, in fact, even to the windlass in her belt, but no longer, thank heavens, our teacher. We watched her spring aboard her motor-boat as it passed us going North, and caught a glimpse of three dazed and vacant faces.

'Drink a lot of beer,' she shouted. It was her last word of advice, but not her last word. Almost out of ear-shot, she lifted her voice again and we heard her faint scream: 'The Blossoms are coming up behind us.'

'I do declare,' said Emma, 'I pity those girls. You can see they think it's hell. Tilly's a marvel, she really is, but she's a killer too if you aren't tough. And those three poor things, by the look of it, ought to be somewhere pretty and soft, far far away from the cut. Nanette, are you smirking over Eli? How sickening you are.'

'The trouble is,' said Charity, hearing, as always, only what she wanted to hear, 'that no one knows a thing about canals till they come on one. People have said to me so many times: "But what do you *do*?" and I can't explain. They seem to think you do nothing but lean on a tiller all day.'

Harry and Leslie had managed to empty the *Venus*. We changed the boats round and they began work, without too much haste, on the *Ariadne*. Emma, suspecting Nanette was sneaking off to clean herself up unfairly, hauled her away to clean the engine instead and help with the clearing out of the mud-box. Charity scrubbed the hatches and tried to clear the disorder to which five days of complete neglect had reduced the butty cabin.

So we were all of us busy and out of sight when the Blossoms went by us. We heard a shout and looking up saw Eli's boots and lower half of his trousers passing the engine-hole doors. Scattering grease-rags, we leapt to our feet and leaned out into his wash. There was Eli, superb and grinning, rather smarter than usual in blue dungarees. His boat seemed to steer herself; twenty years of instinct was in his touch on the tiller-handle. He hardly bothered to glance ahead.

'I knew you was here,' he said. 'Seen Tilly?'

'She went by us half an hour ago. Where are you going to tie?'

'Fishery,' said Eli, mentioning a tie-up some five locks further on.

His Dad lifted his hand as he bicycled past on the tow-path. His fat old Mum, steering the butty, had nothing to say but

216

seemed just as pleased to see us as Eli. We watched them out of sight.

'If that isn't a perfectly beastly shame,' said Nanette. 'Lovely friends and we never see them, except for half a minute like that. What a waste. It's the worst part of this life.'

'I dare say it's all for the best,' said Emma. 'If we saw them more often they might not be our friends.'

'Oh, you are stuffy. I might have known you'd say something pompous like that. I like them, that's all, and there they go.' She waved her hand tragically out of the engine-hole, and picked up a grease-rag, sighing.

But we underrated Eli's staunchness. Harry and Leslie had taken all the coal out of our boats, signed our trip-card, cracked a joke or two and gone home to supper. The butty cabin was a miniature model home. The mud-box had been emptied. The engine-hole was gleaming. We were just beginning tiredly to prise up the floor-boards in the empty holds, meaning to clean the bilges underneath of coal-dust and muck, when there was a whistle from the tow-path on the other side of the cut. We looked across, and there was Eli.

He had bicycled the several miles back to us. His hair was combed flat. He wore a clean scarf round his neck. His ears had been washed. In short, he appeared as a comely young man and a happy surprise, and was very well aware of being both.

Nanette tripped away to the bridge to meet her swain, leaving us to turn half-heartedly back to our task. We found ourselves wishing that three Eli's had whistled across the cut, not one. It was the wrong sort of evening for floor-boards. The bilges were unattractive. We laboured on, becoming dirtier and more silent. Nanette returned, with Eli wheeling his bicycle behind her. She leaned into the hold and whispered to Emma:

'He's asked me to go to the pictures again.'

Emma smeared her face with the back of her hand. 'And what have you said?'

'I've said we'll *all* go with him,' replied Nanette in triumph. 'That makes it quite all right doesn't it? He couldn't be courting three of us at once.'

So the bilges were abandoned. We washed the parts of us that showed, locked up the cabins and caught a bus with Eli. He seemed to be quite unembarrassed at finding himself the escort of three girls instead of one. He liked girls, and he understood girls liked him. That was enough: the evening began with success. We flattered Eli preposterously, laughed at him when he boasted, agreed with him when he lied, admired him both behind his back and before his face and had no quarrel amongst ourselves. The film we saw was appalling and must have been quite unintelligible to Eli. It was America's favourite story of divorce and newspaper men, and we all enjoyed it.

'Frost to-night,' said Eli, as we came out into the dark street. He sniffed the air wisely. 'If I was you,' he said, 'I'd put a lamp in the engine-'ole afore you git to bed.'

He led us straight to a fish-and-chip shop and here we stuffed ourselves fat on grease and potatoes. A short walk shook it all down inside us and made room for a pint or so of beer. As we drank together, Eli told us stories of his very early days and upbringing; of his first attempts at courting; of his friends and enemies on the cut. Though he talked so liberally about himself he showed no interest whatever in our private histories. Except for one question, which he put to each of us in turn – had we any brothers or sisters, and if so, how many? – he asked us nothing, and it was not politeness that prevented him but a complete inability to conceive of any home-life away from the cut. He told us what he had done in the past, or of what others had done to him, but of his ambitions, his intentions, or his wishes, he uttered not a word. In a crude attempt to intellectualize our harmless acquaintanceship we pressed him for opinions and found him disappointing. He thought none of the thoughts we wanted him to think. A doubt

218

crept into our minds that he thought at all. Had we been honest with ourselves, which we were not, we should have admitted that after an hour or so we found him boring. We could not know that it would take a number of years to bring us even within range of a real friendship with Eli; not until the first simplicity of childhood, lost about the age of ten, should be recovered through a difficult wisdom, was it possible for us to understand Eli, and to find him satisfactory.

However, we put him on his bicycle at half past ten and shouted him on his way with many good-nights, and when he had gone declared to one another what a sweet and handsome boy he was – true enough, though we were not altogether sincere in saying so. In any case, he was right about the frost. The air stung our faces. We could read our breaths before us in the starlight. We were wide awake, subtly excited. Bed seemed a commonplace. We stirred up the fire and put a kettle on for a last cup of tea, and, waiting for it to boil, we talked of Wilfred. Nanette topped off the whole conversation with the following remark:

'I don't know,' she said, 'that I miss Wilfred exactly, but I do miss having a man aboard. It's unnatural, at our age, to be cut off from men. We're women, though you mightn't think it to look at us; we need them. Women do.'

The moment the words were out of her mouth, we were over the border: where were our men? We sat in silence before a half-dead fire, groping dimly forward into the weeks of that year, and more dimly into the months of the year to come. We saw ourselves, out of the schoolroom and undiscovered, standing mistily between the deep sea of adolescence and the devil we wanted to know. Where was he? The world had been too noisy recently to hear the little tapping on the insides of our egg-shells. No one knew of us, no one knew we were women; we had only just discovered it ourselves – Nanette had told us. We should have to shout at the tops of our voices to make ourselves heard, but what should we shout? It was half past eleven o'clock. Where were our men, these men? The fire was crumbling. But where, oh where? Notice us! Notice us! was our silent cry. And out of the rubbish of dreams that filled our heads we began busily to form a few exquisite plans.

18

The world was white. The boats were rimed. The heaps of coal were delicate with frost. Sunshine abounded, making the birds' voices into shafts of sound and the road of water metallic. We breakfasted in a flood of bright air, wreathed in the lazy contortions of steam and smoke. Indulgence, a mixture of contentment and impatience, signed the lovely morning. We lingered over cigarettes, allowing our energy to lie coiled inside us for a few more minutes. The world was empty. The boats were white. And we were nearly home.

Before starting off we finished cleaning the bilges. We scraped the disgusting muck into buckets and rinsed it overboard. Then one by one we replaced the floor-boards, stamping them down to make them fit together tightly, and lastly we swept the holds with brooms.

'It would be a pleasure to eat my dinner off those boards,' said Nanette, looking with pride at her handiwork. 'Why, they're cleaner than us.'

We started the engine with practised ease. We cast off the ropes, and the boats were moving forward.

Never had a morning been so brilliant. We left the factories behind us and came again into country where the trees were swelling. We nearly broke the paddles with the vigour of our winding. The boats were winged and tossed a trail of foam behind like angels scattering feathers as they flew. The old

221

stone bridges were studded with jewels that might have been moss. The banks were studded with fishermen and the fishermen picked out from the canal little pieces of mica no bigger than minnows. Through the silver scenery floated swans and willow trees. Our brasses were polished to imitate gold. Our cabintops were slopped and mopped till the blue paint was a bold mockery of the pale sky. Up rose the herons from their long grasses, up curled the creamy smoke from our chimneys. We bared our arms to acknowledge the sun, and covered them hurriedly again, for the air was biting in spite of its radiance. We sang, and the engine was louder, and the deep bubbling of water round the propeller a better tune.

Then we met the Bloweys, and the trip ended with a fight and the fight ended in victory. They were a family of haters. Hate disfigured their faces like small-pox. They hated everyone on the cut and since Nanette had run into their boats on the journey up, and called Mrs. Blowey a silly old prune, they hated us worse than anyone else in the world. Mrs. Blowey, five foot of wizened bale, was the boss of her family. Her two daughters, scowling lumpish girls, were in no way beautified by their names, Ruth and Gloria. Mr. Blowey steered the motor-boat every day of the month and kept his mouth shut.

Ruth Blowey and Nanette, lock-wheeling from opposite directions, arrived at our last lock simultaneously. The lock was full and ready for us. Ruth Blowey showed an inclination to empty the water and make it ready for her boats. Nanette rightly insisted that the lock was ours and refused to let it be stolen by Miss Blowey. The two girls, one at either end of the lock, waited for their respective boats to arrive on the scene, Nanette praying in her heart that we should be the first. We were, by about one minute. As we went into the lock the Blowey boats came into sight round the lower bend and were forced to draw up under the closed gates and wait. Though no doubt irritating for them, all this was in order, and had the short strap towing the butty not broken just as we were beginning to leave the lock, there would have been no incident. However, break it did, at that exact moment, and so gave rise to the now famous battle.

There was one impartial witness. Boats were on our tail and a lock-wheeler bicycled up behind us just in time to enjoy the following five minutes. No blood was shed, but the story got round as a bloody one, and this was due to him and his feeling for drama.

The rope snapped and the *Venus* skimmed ahead; the butty remained where she was, cumbering up the lock. It took a little time to check the motor in her headlong career and bring her back astern to pick up her sister. The Bloweys had a grievance: we were holding them up.

While the lock-wheeler leaned over his bicycle, Emma and Charity struggled to improvise a new short strap, and Nanette hovered on the tow-path, Mrs. Blowey stood up on the bows of her motor-boat and at the top of her raucous voice told us what she thought of us. The other Bloweys listened in morose approval. Abuse poured out of her mouth without a comma dividing it. Some of the words we understood as being filthy, but she used a good many new and interesting ones at whose filth we could only guess. Emma began to blush with anger. Nanette on the tow-path began to laugh.

Gloria whirled round. The fury in her face was lunatic. 'Shut that,' she screamed, and we had them at once at our mercy. Laughter was more than they could bear; it was poison, we could choke them with it. So we laughed, half in hate, as loudly as we could, and it was nearly the end of Nanette. For Gloria Blowey snatched up a short shaft lying on the cabin-top in front of her and hurled it like a javelin straight for Nanette's head, a few feet away. On the end of every shaft is a boat-hook. Nanette ducked and it sailed over her shoulder.

We stopped laughing. Mrs. Blowey had stopped screaming. We were too far away to help Nanette, for our own boats had drifted by this time out of the lock and were lying in the middle of the cut with the Bloweys' boats between us and the tow-path. Nanette acted as heroines do, on the impulse. She picked up the shaft and flung it straight back, with a good aim for Gloria's ugly face. Mr. Blowey, otherwise a lay figure, made his only move: he lifted one arm, fielded the shaft very neatly in mid-air, and laid it back on the cabin-top. We began to feel hysterical and let out a cheer, intended for Nanette. She was in need of support more substantial than cheering, for Ruth Blowey was rushing down from the lock-side like a bitch gone mad, rolling up her sleeves and yelling. We knew Nanette was terrified. We had never thought of her as being intrepid. We expected to see her turn and fly from this horrible girl as fast as she could. Nothing of the kind. Instead, we beheld her roll up her own sleeves and double her fists, and heard her squeak out:

'All right – I'm not afraid of you.'

The Bloweys were beaten. For if Nanette was a coward and hid it, Ruth Blowey was six times as great a coward and showed it in a moment. She pulled up short, dropped her arms and slunk stupidly away. That was the end. We had won. The lock-wheeler was grinning with pleasure. We picked up our brave Nanette at the next bridge-hole and made a tremendous fuss of her.

'I was so frightened,' she said, 'I was nearly being sick. I thought they were sure to kill me. I would have run away but I'm such a bad runner.'

We were jubilant, so proud of her that she soon became proud of herself. The frosty trees flew by. A saw-mill passed us on the left-hand side and a chocolate factory on the right. The day was white with glory. The glory was ours and the day was ours and the depot rushed to meet us.

There were the sprawling buildings, the sheds and tin roofs. There was the lay-by, and above the sound of the engine we thought we heard a hammering and a buzz of life. There was the oil-shop, there was the repairing-yard, and there, tied outside the dry-dock, was a pair of boats we recognized with a figure standing up on the bows, looking towards us like a welcome.

'Why, I believe it's that awful little Amos,' cried Charity joyfully, and we all began waving.

Emma is the girl front right of this 1944 publicity photograph which is largely phoney. It's taken near the GUC Hayes Depot, Middlesex and the boats are real enough, but a small amount of cargo has been planted in an otherwise empty hold; we are only pretending to tie the rolled-down side-cloths; and moreover, if we were genuinely working Emma would most probably be barefoot and wearing dungarees – *not* a skirt and sandals!

A NOTE ON THE AUTHOR

Emma Smith was born Elspeth Hallsmith in 1923 in Newquay, Cornwall, where she lived until the age of twelve. Her first book, *Maidens' Trip*, was published in 1948 and won the John Llewellyn Rhys Memorial Prize. Her second, *The Far Cry*, was published the following year and was awarded the James Tait Black Memorial Prize.

In 1951 Emma Smith married Richard Stewart-Jones. After her husband's death in 1957 she went to live with her two young children in Wales, where she proceeded to write four successful children's books, a number of short stories and, in 1978, her novel *The Opportunity of a Lifetime*. In 2008 her memoir of her Cornish childhood, *The Great Western Beach*, was published to widespread critical acclaim. Emma has lived in the London district of Putney since 1980.

A NOTE ON THE TYPE

The text of this book is set in Linotype Sabon, named after
the type founder, Jacques Sabon. It was designed by Jan
Tschichold and jointly developed by Linotype, Monotype
and Stempel, in response to a need for a typeface to be
available in identical form for mechanical hot metal
composition and hand composition using foundry type.

Tschichold based his design for Sabon roman on a font
engraved by Garamond, and Sabon italic on a font by
Granjon. It was first used in 1966 and has proved
an enduring modern classic.